Abou

Born in 1938, Jeremy Dix experienced the wartime years in rural Wiltshire. He was educated at Devizes Grammar School and the Bishop Wordsworth's School, Salisbury, where his English teacher was William Golding. After teacher training at St Paul's Cheltenham (1958-1961), he taught at Corsham and Watford, before entering local government in leisure management, serving Kingston upon Hull City Council and then North Wiltshire District, before retirement. A keen Rotarian, his hobbies include watercolour painting, photography, gardening, golf and walking the dog.

Operation Wansdyke

Jeremy Dix

Operation Wansdyke

Vanguard Press

ISBN 978 1 784653 12 5

*Vanguard Press is an imprint of
Pegasus Elliot Mackenzie Publishers Ltd.*
www.pegasuspublishers.com

First Published in 2017

**Vanguard Press
Sheraton House Castle Park
Cambridge England**
Printed & Bound in Great Britain

Dedication

This is for Sue and Sally, my greatest and most helpful critics, for their help and support.

In memory of Mum and Dad, the best parents ever.

Chapter One

The unmarked aircraft dropped below the cloud base at fifteen hundred feet, banked to the right and throttled back, the pilot searching for the grass runway in the black night.

The engine noise was replaced by the whistling of the slipstream over the wing struts and of rain rattling on the cockpit as the plane began its steep glide down to its destination.

The three passengers strained to look out of the side screens through the rain for any recognisable landmark which might confirm their location.

Two of the passengers, a man and a woman, wore civilian clothing – the woman's hand wrapped in blood-stained bandaging – while the third passenger, a man, wore the distinctive uniform of a German Oberst of the Waffen SS.

Suddenly, they could make out the lambing pens on the remote, windswept downs below them and then they were crossing over the Devizes to Beckhampton road.

At that same moment the pilot called out in relief, "I've got it! Hold tight! This could be rather bumpy!"

Ahead, he could now make out the narrow grass strip at the end of which he knew there stood a large, black barn, its sliding doors pulled wide open.

From the protection of the barn's interior, two headlights flashed a welcome towards the plane as it made its final decent. The pilot flared expertly and brought the plane to a bumpy stop. Then, with a final burst of throttle, he rolled it neatly to a halt inside the barn itself.

The guiding car headlights were immediately doused and shadowy figures ran to close the barn doors. A moment of silence followed, broken only by the clicking of cooling hot metal.

Abruptly, the plane door was wrenched open and the passengers, followed by the pilot, stepped gingerly out onto the ground, stretching their cramped limbs.

The plane's occupants shook hands with the welcoming party before they clambered stiffly into the car and were driven away through the rain towards the nearby remote farmstead, secreted behind a dense windbreak of beech trees, leaving behind two ground crew to re-rig the camouflage netting around the barn doors to protect it from prying eyes.

What they didn't know was that, on this night, two pairs of prying eyes had witnessed everything.

Chapter Two

The village of Barton Cannings was having a good war.

Sitting in isolation at the foot of the Marlborough Downs, it had, so far, avoided the attention of the Luftwaffe.

Furthermore, despite rationing restrictions, food was relatively plentiful, thanks to the produce of gardens and the allotments. The "Dig for Victory" posters were patriotically observed by everyone – and most people kept a few chickens, so poultry and eggs were available. Meat, however, was strictly rationed and was only available from the butchers in Devizes, although Jeff Stevens could be relied on for a rabbit for the pot and milk was usually (and illegally) available from the dairy at Chambers' farm for making extra butter.

If anything, the village economy had seen an upturn. The Crown Inn and Jones' shop and bakery were both grateful for the extra custom provided by soldiers from the nearby Le Marchant garrison (although, strictly speaking, the village was off-limits to army personnel) and, when the American camp and military hospital had arrived in 1942, village residents relished the prospect of even more trade – not to mention extra supplies of American goods.

So, for day-to-day existence, the village was almost self-reliant, except for purchasing hardware, for visits to the doctors and the barbers. For these, a journey to nearby Devizes was necessary, involving a three-mile bike ride. The few villagers who had vehicles and the necessary petrol coupons would go by car, some used pony and trap while an unreliable bus service sometimes ran on Thursdays to coincide with the weekly market.

Other essentials were still brought to Barton Cannings by van or carrier. Fred Burt's oil van called weekly from Devizes with paraffin for oil lamps and cooking stoves and, from the Edwards' van, villagers exchanged newly-charged acid accumulators for their old ones in order to keep their wirelesses working to listen to news bulletins, to ITMA and to Henry Hall.

At less regular intervals, coal and anthracite was delivered on Mr Angel's coal lorry.

However, the War had irreversibly changed village life. Many of the menfolk were away, serving overseas, while the rest of the community had long since adjusted to Britain being on a war footing.

Mrs Cully and Mrs Eden had both taken in refugee children from London.

Mr and Mrs Jenks were billeting two army officers.

Arthur Kemp (RN retired) had been appointed ARP (Air Raid Precaution) warden although, in the absence of any air raids, he occupied his time patrolling the village on his creaking bicycle, checking there were no chinks of light escaping around the edge of anyone's blacked-out windows. He had arranged the issue of gas masks to everyone in cardboard boxes held by a string shoulder strap with instructions that they should be carried at all times. However, when it became apparent that the village was unlikely to be the target of any German bombing mission, few people bothered to carry them – and some small boys had found the boxes ideal for holding collections of birds' eggs.

Scanton's family funfair had taken up residence in a field next to the school, the exciting chair plane and dodgem rides now all mothballed. The huge lorries, caravans, the steam traction engine and generator, which formed part of the once-proud Scanton empire, were dotted around the edge of the field. Stinging nettles were beginning to grow up through some of the machinery and the paintwork was faded and peeling. Some of the men from the extensive Scanton family were away, fighting in the deserts of North Africa, while Gran Scanton governed over the remainder of her clan from her spotless showman's caravan,.

Barry Dyke, headmaster of the small, all-age school (just three classes) was having a difficult time in curbing the natural excitement of his younger pupils, who regarded the arrival of army tanks and lorries and the overhead flights of bombers and fighter planes with great enthusiasm. There were few youngsters who couldn't tell a Hurricane from a Spitfire and most of them recognised the Lancaster, Mosquito and the other bombers which regularly flew over the village.

Boys would run around the playground, arms outstretched like wings, imitating aerial combat and emitting noises like machine-gun fire, followed by the sounds of explosions, as their bombs rained down.

Sometimes boys found strips of bright aluminium foil hanging in festoons in the trees and hedges. These strips were highly prized and were attached to bicycle handlebars as souvenirs, although it was never explained to them that this was "window" of "chaff" which had been dropped by German bombers to confuse British radar plotters.

The pupils had all been warned of the dangers of talking to strangers and of accepting presents. The senior girls had been particularly warned on the perils of flirting with army personnel – especially with Americans who, it was widely rumoured, had endless supplies of nylon stockings, chewing gum and cigarettes to fraternise with the locals and sufficient to entice the flowers of the village to part with their virginity.

Strangely, this warning seemed to have had the opposite to the desired effect and, for some of the more daring girls, the hay barn at Chambers' farm was a popular destination for weekend sexual adventures. However, there were two teenage girls who were now wishing they'd heeded that advice; Jane Ward was now pushing a pram and Rosie Hill was heavily pregnant.

Their plight was the topic of conversation at the village post office, which was housed in the converted front room of a thatched cottage in Chandler's Lane, named "Old Roses".

Postmistress Edie Jessop was often the first to pick up gossip. She was also the first to pronounce her judgement on any subject to anyone in the post office queue who cared to listen – and that didn't give much option for those who were waiting to be served in the cramped room.

"Those two girls lay on their backs for anything that wore trousers, they did! I'd always said that they were asking for trouble, didn't I, Dot?" she said over her shoulder to her sister, who was emptying the contents of the post box into a grubby mailbag.

Pink-faced from her exertions, Dot stood up, blinking. "You did, Edie. You did!" she readily agreed. It seems that Dot had agreed with her elder sister for her entire fifty-eight years.

"Well," continued Edie, seamlessly ignoring her sibling's practiced loyalty, "now they'll have to make the best of it. That's what I say!"

"They will. They will!" agreed Dot, straightening the glasses which had slid down her nose.

The sisters were both tall and very upright. Dot, now a widow of some four years, was a little plumper than Edie, who enjoyed her authority in the position of postmistress. She was a spinster and was resigned to the fact – and her waspish tongue, scrawny looks and prim clothing seemed likely to ensure her prospects in this regard wouldn't change.

Edie suddenly banged her stamp into the black ink pad on the counter and franked three letters with such ferocity that the small boy who had brought them flinched with surprise.

She leaned menacingly over the counter and gave the boy what she thought was a winning smile. "You can tell you mother these will go in the five o'clock collection, Cyril," she told him loudly, presuming that the volume of her voice would increase his understanding.

He nodded quickly and gratefully scuttled out of the door.

"Mind you," Edie announced to the remainder of the queue, as she critically examined a small package presented by the next customer, "I can't say as that bringing that girls' school into the village makes any sense. First we have to put up with a fair being dumped on us and now it's a school! Why they couldn't have gone to a place in Swindon or Devizes beats me! There's so much more suitable property there. Much more suitable!"

"Yes, much more suitable," echoed Dot, meekly.

With the delivery of the Jessop verdict on the new arrivals, silence descended, broken only by the ticking of the post office clock and the periodic thump of Edie's franking. The queuing customers appeared reluctant to express an opinion, let alone disagree.

Eventually, Mrs Stagg summoned up courage.

"But that school – they was bombed out, poor things. Wasn't they? Our Stan reckons we got to 'elp where we can. It's not as though they'm being a nuisance, is they?"

She immediately wished she'd said nothing, knowing the delay that another Jessop sermon could cause, and she wasn't to be disappointed.

With exaggerated deliberation Edie replaced a package she was holding onto the counter, adjusted her glasses, closed her eyes in exasperation and leant forward on two straight arms – much as she had seen the Reverend Blunt do at church.

"That's as may be, Rachel, so long as they stay inside Lynton House" – she emphasised *inside* – "but I can't see those girls being cooped up there for too long before they'll want more space. You mark my words. And *then* what's going to happen? They'll be all over the village. They've already had to convert stables at the back into more classrooms."

Edie franked the package.

Rachel Stagg thought to say that the creation of two cleaning jobs at Lynton House had been most welcome, and then thought better of countering Edie's views.

"As for those Scantons," Edie continued, "they're *fair* people!" Her delivery implied this was a damning indictment enough. "Mark my words! It's only a matter of time before those young scallywags get into trouble!"

And, throughout this monologue, Dot had had difficulty in deciding which bit of her sister's outburst to support and so stayed silent, while the remaining members of the queue, which had been joined by a young woman with a bandaged hand, waited patiently to be served.

The arrival of the St Hilda's Boarding School for Girls had certainly caused a stir in the village. The school's buildings in Aldgate had taken a direct hit in a bombing raid on London. Luckily, this was during the half-term holiday, so the premises had been empty at the time, except for the caretaker, and he'd survived because, at the time, he'd been sampling a pint at the nearby Nag's Head.

After sifting through the wreckage to salvage valuable textbooks, the school had been instructed to leave London and, at short notice, it had been relocated to Lynton House, Barton Cannings' most prominent building, as its new home.

So, sixty-eight pupils (headmistress, Dr Patricia Madely, referred to them as "her young ladies") accompanied by five teachers, two cooks and the caretaker had all arrived at Devizes station after a tortuous journey in a train full of troops, before being taken to their destination in two coaches.

"Ladies," Dr Madely had addressed her charges on their arrival, crammed into the large dining room, "we are most fortunate to have been evacuated to this charming village. It may not be *quite* what we've been used to, and it may lack the sophistication we normally expect, but I want you all to look upon this experience as an opportunity to broaden your horizons in this rural setting. So, continue to behave like ladies. No talking to the local boys... and *do* be careful where you put your feet when we go out on our nature rambles! I believe they have cows here."

That had been three months ago and now the school had settled into its new premises as best it could. The village was getting used to seeing columns of pupils, with their gas masks slung from their shoulders, walking along its narrow lanes under the watchful eyes of teachers, Misses Clarke and Phelps, who gave withering glares at any of the local boys who dared to gawp in open admiration at the girls as they filed past.

Pupils and staff now attended church each Sunday morning and the Reverend Blunt had been delighted to have his congregation grow so abruptly. He had failed to see any connection between this and a simultaneous growth of interest from boys wanting to join the choir – most of them with voices which had broken long ago.

Games lessons for the pupils consisted of gentle ball games on the spacious lawns in front of the house when the weather permitted. When, in Dr Madely's judgement, it was too cold for the girls to wear their gym slips, they would be wrapped up in scarves, coats and hats and they'd set off on long nature rambles across the neighbouring fields and beside the nearby canal.

After three months of struggling to cope with the academic and the pastoral demands made by her pupils, Dr Madely was both relieved and excited with the arrival of the three new additions to her staff and she introduced them in the small staffroom during a morning break.

"Ladies," she looked at Miss Clarke and Miss Phelps, "Mr Gloyne, I want to introduce you to your new colleagues who are joining us today."

"Firstly, I'd like you to meet Dawn Crosby, who will be taking over Biology and Games. Miss Crosby hails from Shrewsbury and I'm sure she's going to make an excellent contribution to the life in our school."

Mr Gloyne, who had been immersed in a Latin primer before Dr Madely's little speech, regarded Dawn Crosby open-mouthed, and hoped that the contribution the headmistress had referred to would involve *him*.

For Dawn Crosby, twenty-four, was stunningly attractive. She had a slim but curvaceous figure, and her dress served to emphasise the excellent proportions of her firm, high breasts, trim waist and pert bottom and it did little to conceal the lines of her long legs. To compliment these features she had dark hair, shining blue eyes and a full mouth which broke into a ready smile as she shook hands with her new colleagues. She moved round the group with a youthful grace, blissfully unaware of the impact her presence was having on the room.

"Next," continued Dr Madely, "please welcome Richard Kymer. Mr Kymer, who joins us from Cheltenham, no less, will be helping Miss Clarke and teaching Modern Languages."

Richard Kymer stood over six feet tall. Although he walked with a slight limp, he was still lithe and athletic-looking. He had dark hair and finely chiselled features. He smiled with an easy charm at his new colleagues and, unlike Dawn Crosby, he was entirely aware of the effect of his charismatic presence. Miss Phelps' heartbeat increased as he bowed curtly to shake her hand. Next came Miss Clarke, who proffered a trembling hand as, again, Kymer gave her a short bow and a beaming smile. Mr Gloyne regarded him enviously, wishing he could wind back the clock to his own early thirties, but made welcoming noises nonetheless as he shook Kymer's hand.

"And finally," cooed Dr Madely, "but certainly not least, please welcome Christine Edwards. Miss Edwards will be helping Miss Phelps with English and she also will be teaching Art. Miss Edwards joins us from Bath."

Dr Madely inclined her head towards Miss Phelps, who she'd hoped would be grateful for the help which had been long promised and was here at last.

Christine Edwards' appearance was in marked contrast to that of Dawn Crosby. Despite her large bust, she had an unmistakeable hardness about her, and this look was accentuated by an altogether masculine hairstyle, which had been cut severely short at the back and sides. Her face was devoid of make-up, her eyebrows were plucked to oblivion and she had pale, thin lips, all of which gave the appearance of her being older than her twenty-nine years.

She smiled as she vigorously pumped the hands of her new colleagues, while Dr Madely stood back to assess the reactions in the room as everyone became acquainted.

"I should mention," explained Dr Madely to her new appointees, "that there are two more colleagues for you to meet who're not here today. Mr Sharples, who teaches Maths and Science, has gone to Devizes to collect a parcel for me from the station. And then there's Mr Jones, who teaches Geography. He's visiting his sick mother in Portsmouth. However, he hopes to be back tomorrow, provided the trains are running."

From the general hubbub of meeting and greeting in the room, it was not clear how much notice had been taken of this last information as the focus of attention was centred on the newcomers.

Predictably, Richard Kymer was making a hit with Miss Phelps, Miss Clarke and Dawn Crosby. Eric Gloyne couldn't take his eyes off Dawn Crosby while Dr Madely noted that Christine Edwards also seemed to be at ease with her new colleagues.

"Mr Kymer," warbled Miss Clarke. "Welcome to St Hilda's. This must be slightly different from teaching in Cheltenham. Had you been there long?"

"Thank you, Miss Clarke," replied Kymer, giving her one of his winning smiles. "Yes, I'd been there nearly five years. Cheltenham is such a beautiful town so I was sad to leave. But I'm sure I'm going to enjoy being here at St Hilda's in this lovely village just as much. For one thing, it'll be a pleasant change to be teaching smaller classes."

"Were you at Cheltenham Ladies College?" asked Miss Phelps, "Dr Madley must have been very persuasive to prise you away from such an important seat of learning!"

"Well, I have to admit it wasn't an easy decision to make but, as you say, Dr Madely can be very persuasive."

Meanwhile, Dawn Crosby, who was standing next to Kymer, was being quizzed by Eric Gloyne. "I used to have an uncle who lived near Shrewsbury – had a farm near the river – always being flooded in the winter. Did you live in the town, Miss Crosby?"

"Do please call me Dawn," she laughed. "No, I lived with my parents who farm at a place called Ford. But I taught in the town."

Miss Clarke, who was slightly miffed that Miss Phelps seemed to have monopolised Richard Kymer's attention, turned to Christine Edwards.

"So, Miss Edwards. What attracted you to join us at St Hilda's?"

"That wasn't a difficult decision to make, really, Miss Clarke. And do call me Chris." She spoke with a much softer tone of voice than her hard appearance may have led Miss Clarke to expect.

"I'd been teaching near Coventry, but I moved to Bath, thinking that it might get me away from the bombing. But, no sooner had I arrived than the city was hit by an air raid and my digs in Upper Bristol Road were flattened."

"How shocking for you," sympathised Miss Clarke. "That must have been a frightful experience!"

"I'll say it was. Very upsetting. So I started looking for a post at a school out in the country, which wasn't easy, under the present circumstances. Then, when I eventually learnt of the vacancy here at St Hilda's, I couldn't believe my luck. So I applied, and here I am!"

"Well, I'm sure you won't regret it. This is a lovely school and most of the children are well-behaved, not to mention the staff!" she added, chuckling at her own joke.

Christine Edwards laughed in appreciation and turned towards Richard Kymer, who was disengaging himself from Miss Phelps' clutches.

"Did I hear you'd been teaching at the Ladies' College, Mr Kymer?"she asked.

"Richard, please. Yes, I did around five years there before I got called up for active service. Then I injured my leg during training at Catterick, after which the army didn't want to know me! So I was invalided out and, after another gap for recuperation, I was fortunate enough to return to Cheltenham."

"Cheltenham's such an attractive place – even the War can't disguise that," she replied. "I expect you had lots of opportunities to get out and explore the area," she added.

"I did!" he enthused. "There was so much to take in and, although I loved the Regency architecture of the town, I think my favourite times were spent walking up on the Cotswold escarpment. You could walk for hours up there and everywhere you looked, there were the most stunning views. From the top of Cleeve Hill, you could look north out over the valley with the whole town spread out below you. You sound as though you know Cheltenham, Miss Edwards. When were you there last?"

"Oh, a couple of years ago. I've only been a few times, but it was enough to leave a lasting impression on me. I used to visit a pal who lived there."

Dr Madely interrupted the flow of conversation to suggest that the newcomers should get settled into their allotted rooms.

"Mr Kymer, I'm afraid I've had to put you in the small box room on the top floor. It's rather cramped, but I think you'll find it very snug. Miss Crosby, you're also on the top floor, next to Mr Gloyne's room and Miss Edwards, you'll find your room on the first floor next to the senior dormitory. As you know, furniture is hard to come by so we've had to move some around to make best use of what we've got. I appreciate it may not be ideal, but we've tried to make you all as comfortable as possible."

Before leaving the staff room, Dr Madely suggested that they join their colleagues at lunch, when there'd be ample time to get more closely acquainted.

Chapter Three

As the conversation in the staffroom at Lynton House grew in volume, below stairs, Ali Jenkins took off her cleaning overall and hung it in the store cupboard having first retrieved her coat and scarf.

She climbed the stone stairs to the hall and, leaving by the front door, she took her bike from by the entrance steps and crunched down the short, gravel drive to the double, wrought-iron entrance gates. She pulled open one of the gates. The hinges squeaked protestingly from lack of oil. She closed the gate behind her and crossed the road. Mounting her bike, she cycled along a narrow lane, then through the churchyard and on to her cottage in Chandlers Lane, which she shared with her invalid mother.

Ali Jenkins was thirty-two years of age and still unmarried, despite having a fine figure and looks which turned the head of most red-blooded men. That is not to say that Ali had never experienced romance. For two years she'd conducted an extremely steamy relationship with Roy Boswell.

Whenever they could, she and Roy would steal upstairs to her room, once her mother had dosed off to sleep after her dinner. There, by the flickering flame of the oil lamp, Roy would silently undress Ali, never tiring at his own delight of seeing Ali's ample breasts pop out from her bra when he removed it. Ali's excitement would intensify as she felt Roy slowly draw down her knickers and then feel his breath on the inside of her thighs as he nibbled his way upwards.

She would then lie back on the bed, propped up on her elbows, and watch while Roy made her wait as he slowly and deliberately undressed, finally to reveal his full erection.

Their lovemaking was intense although, throughout, they had always to avoid waking Ali's mother as they writhed together towards their climax. Later, panting and content, they clung to each other for some time and eventually relaxed in the warm, tingling glow of mutual satisfaction. Then, as silently as they had arrived, they would dress and tiptoe down the stairs to the kitchen, where Ali would make a drink of cocoa for her mother, before she was put to bed, while Roy would slip out of the side door into the night.

Ali and Roy had talked of marriage and had started to make tentative plans – but then the War came. Like many young men from the village, Roy had received his call-up papers and, within three weeks, he'd been posted to Plymouth, where he embarked as a rating on *HMS Exeter*. That had been fourteen months ago and Ali hadn't heard from him since, except for a censored postcard she'd received back in November.

Ali parked her bike in the lean-to shed beside the cottage and opened the door into the kitchen. "It's me, mum," she called through to the lounge, as she removed her coat and scarf. "I'm home."

Frances Jenkins had been snoozing in her chair in front of the cooking range when Ali called out. The drugs prescribed by Dr Sayers were helping to deaden the pain in her arthritic hips but they were inclined to make her drowsy in the warmth of the snug lounge.

Ali filled the kettle and took it through to the cooking range where she placed it on the boiler ring, before giving the fire a poke and opening the damper to draw the flames. She kissed her mother on the forehead.

"How are you feeling, Mum? Let's get you nice and comfy," she added, tucking her mother's blanket round her legs. "There! That's better," she said, giving her knees an affectionate pat. "Had any callers today?"

Frances Jenkins hated being a burden on her attractive daughter but blessed her for the unconditional love and care that Ali gave her. She knew only too well the sacrifice that Ali was making and hoped that, somehow, in spite of "all of this war business", Ali might still find a nice young man to "walk out with", totally unaware of Ali's own hope that Roy would eventually return home safely.

Frances smiled her thanks for Ali's fussing over her. "Now, Alison. Tell me all about how the new job's going? You must be worn out."

"Actually, it wasn't too bad. They've given me a nice overall and all the mops and polishes I could possibly need. The work itself is pretty easy really, although, when those little blighters traipsed in from Games and trampled all over my nice, polished floor, I felt I could throttle them!"

Mrs Jenkins smiled a sympathetic smile and, at this point, the kettle started to sing and Ali went to the kitchen and returned with a tea tray.

"Oh, yes, Ali," she remembered, "I *did* have a visitor. A nice man called this morning – not long after Mr Hudd delivered the milk. At first I thought he was going to try to sell me something and then I realised he wanted to speak to you. A middle-aged gentleman, he was, and he had a sort of military presence. You know – rather a posh voice, very abrupt speaking," Frances paused in recollection. "But he seemed a nice enough bloke." Another pause.

"Well, we chatted for some time. He seemed to be a keen gardener. I think he'd noticed all of your efforts in the border and I told him about how much time you spend out there in the potting shed."

Ali knew that her mother had a number of visitors during the week – usually arranged through the Reverend Blunt – kind people, who would read the single-sheet newspaper to her, do little jobs and keep her company. So Ali hadn't been particularly surprised to hear of France's most recent caller until, that is, she realised that the visitor hadn't called on Frances but that he had wanted to speak to her.

"Anyway," Frances continued, "he seemed a bit vague about why he'd called. I think he must have been from Horton garden club because he asked me to be sure to tell you that Juliet Oscar had brought out a new seeds catalogue."

Ali started and her heart gave a lurch, although she succeeded in controlling her voice to ask as casually as she could, "Mum, can you remember what his exact words were?"

"Oh, yes. He said I was to tell you that Juliet Oscar had brought out a new seeds catalogue in November and that he was sure you'd find that interesting. I thought it was unusual because they usually bring them out in the spring."

"Did he say anything else? Did he tell you who he was, for instance?"

She poured the tea as she listened to her mother's answer.

"No, I thought at the time that that was a bit strange – but I didn't like to ask. From the way he chatted, I just gathered that he knew you."

Ali beamed at Frances and patted her hand. "Thank you, Mum. That's very helpful and I think you're right. He must have been from the garden club. They've got so many new members, I find it difficult to remember who they all are, myself. And my seed catalogue is getting a bit frayed so, next time I'm in Devizes, I'll call in at Catleys and get a copy. Now, if you're quite comfy, I'll pop out to the shed to see how my next batch of plants is coming on."

Giving France's hand a final squeeze, Ali went out to her potting shed at the back of the cottage. The weathered shed door was secured with a large, rusting padlock thrust through an equally rusty, heavy duty hasp and staple. With trembling fingers, Ali unlocked the padlock, opened the door and went in, pulling the door to behind her and securing it from inside.

Next, she checked that the grubby net curtains completely covered the small window and turned her attention to the work bench, which was covered in an array of wooden seed trays, clay pots of various sizes, a trowel and dibbers. There were four seed trays which already contained compost and these Ali carefully slid to one side to expose the flat work surface, into which was fitted a concealed panel, hinged on one side. She carefully brushed loose soil off the panel, felt beneath the work top for the hidden button and pressed. With a small clunk, the edge of the panel sprang up and Ali was able to raise it on its hinges to reveal, in a shallow recess below, a short wave radio transceiver, a Morse key and earphones. At the side of the radio were a number of thin files, some papers written in German and an automatic pistol.

She lifted out one of the files and opened the first page, looking for the list of message codes.

She ran her finger down the page over a list of initial letters. "Juliet Oscar November," she whispered, barely able to contain her excitement, "Juliet Oscar November, where are you? Ah! Here it is!" she said, stabbing her finger on the initials J O N. She briefly checked the entry beside the initials, flapped the file shut and returned it to the recess. The panel was then closed with a click. She sprinkled soil over the working surface and returned the seed trays to their original positions, before finally checking her handiwork to ensure everything looked normal.

Ali came out of the shed and secured the door carefully behind her and ran back into the cottage to collect her coat.

"Mum, I'm going to the phone box to make a call. I shouldn't be too long." So saying, she retrieved her bike from the lean-to and headed off in the gloaming towards the village centre.

Barton Cannings, like many Wiltshire villages, hadn't been connected to the telephone network until the late 1930s and, so far, only a few houses had taken advantage of its arrival.

Consequently, most residents relied on the only public telephone kiosk in the village for making their calls, and this was located in Chandlers Lane, close to the Crown Inn.

As Ali approached the kiosk she saw, to her annoyance, that it was already occupied. So, stopping some twenty paces away, she lifted her bike up onto the grass verge and parked it against the hedge and prepared to wait.

However, her wait was a short one since the occupant left the kiosk in an apparent hurry and walked briskly away from her in the direction of the pub.

There was just sufficient light for Ali to check her watch and, to her relief, she saw that it was two minutes to four. She pulled hard to open the kiosk's sprung door and entered. It was difficult to see but, for what Ali had been briefed to do, this posed little problem.

At exactly four o'clock, Ali lifted the hand set from its cradle and dialled four digits, inserted her three pence, and then replaced the phone and waited.

After only a matter of seconds, the phone started ringing and, following her instructions, Ali let it ring four times before she lifted the receiver and pushed button A and pressed the phone to her ear with trembling hands.

"Your identification code?" demanded a man's voice, metallic sounding and rather threatening.

"Apple, Mike, Juliet, two, zero, one," she responded, using the phonetics as she'd been taught. There was a slight pause, before another voice spoke – more gentle and cultured, but nonetheless authoritative.

"Be at the intersection of London Road with the Calne road at 1930 hours this evening where a car will meet you. Your response to the driver will be *Roundway*. Have you understood that?"

"Yes. 1930 hours on London road. My response is *Roundway*."

"Thank you. Good evening." And, before Ali could say anything else, the line went dead.

Ali left the kiosk in a mixed state of excitement and apprehension, her mind a confused jumble of questions and suppositions. Where was she being taken? What had come up that required her to break her cover?

With this mêlée of thoughts in her mind, she returned home, wondering how she was going to explain away her absence to her mother, not knowing when she'd be back. In the end she fell back on a limp excuse.

"Mum, I'm going to the Horton gardening club," she lied, as she walked into the parlour. "They've got a special spring meeting tonight which might go on some time, so there's no need for you to wait up for me. I'll make you a nice cup of cocoa to take to bed with you before I go."

Frances gave her daughter an appreciative smile.

"That's all right, my dear. You go to your meeting. I'm expecting Rachel Stagg round later so I won't be on my own. Mind you wrap up warm, though. It looks like it's going to be cold tonight."

Chapter Four

Hattie Perkins had been the cook at St Hilda's for over thirteen years and she was regarded as something of an institution. So, although she was obviously expected to meet the requirements of her employers, it was generally accepted that Hattie carried out her duties as she saw fit and no one – not even Dr Madely – dared to interfere in Hattie's domain of the kitchen or the laundry.

Jovial and plump, she had seen many changes of both faces and fortunes during her years of service. Certainly, there had been a steady turnover of staff during her time as cook and she had her own views on the present occupants of the staffroom and she quickly formed an opinion on any newcomers.

As for the school's fortunes, she was resigned to the fluctuations that followed St Hilda's in the competitive world of private education. Numbers on the school roll would fall and rise and Hattie had always been convinced that the healthy diet she was able to offer was a strong selling point for Dr Madely when meeting prospective parents.

Of course the war, with its food shortages and rationing, had posed Hattie with new challenges but, despite these, she developed a knack of producing appetising food using the most basic ingredients available from the girls' ration books – much to the satisfaction of the headmistress.

On this particular Saturday afternoon, Hattie was preparing tea for the girls. Some of them were having an extra Art lesson with Chris Edwards while the group of seniors, who had been taken out for a cross-country run by Dawn Crosby, would soon be returning. The menu, a shepherd's pie made from corned beef accompanied by locally produced vegetables to be followed by bread-and-butter pudding, was in the final stages of preparation and, as she looked out the kitchen window, she saw the tall figure of Richard Kymer limp past.

Daisy Tonks, who helped Hattie at weekends, saw him, too.

"That Mr Kymer. He does get about. It seems he's always out walking," she concluded. "Only last week I was out with our dog and I seen him creeping out of the tree plantation at the back of the American camp."

"I'm not surprised," replied Hattie. "He says he likes to go exploring – although what there is to explore around here beats me. I think he just prefers his own company. Spends a lot of his time up there in his room after his walks, he does. The airing cupboard is just next door and many's the time I've been getting out the clean linen when I've heard him tapping away."

"Mind you," added Daisy, "he's not the only one who gets out an' about. My Frank says as he's seen our Mr Sharples at The Crown on occasions. Each time 'e were talking with this swarthy character. Frank's mates reckon 'e was from Devizes. He always 'as 'is car parked outside, so he must have come from Devizes."

Daisy lowered her voice to a conspiratorial whisper, as though to avoid being overheard.

"D'you know! They'd sit in a corner on their own, as though they didn't want any interruptions. Just talking. An' when they'd finished, this bloke would up an' leave Mr Sharples to finish his drink on his own."

Although the staff shared the lofty dining room with the pupils, they ate at a separate table and they were able to talk without fear of being overheard.

As they gathered later for high tea, there was general, wide-ranging conversation – Churchill's latest radio broadcast, the mess left on the road by the herd of cows at Court Farm, the new gas mask regulations...

"Did I see you out for another walk today, Richard?" enquired Chris Edwards.

"Yes, you did," he replied, with his usual charming smile. "This little place is astonishing, you know, and there's so much to see here."

"There can't be many places around the village that you haven't been to," she teased. "Where did you get to this time?"

"Oh, just out and about – nowhere in particular. I just enjoy following my nose. What about you, Dawn? Did you enjoy your run with the girls?" he flashed a smile across the table to where Dawn Crosby was tucking in to her shepherd's pie.

"Yes, I did. In fact, we had quite an adventure! We had jogged along Chandlers Lane to the Bridge Inn and I had hoped to take the canal towpath towards Devizes." She took another mouthful of shepherd's pie.

"I've walked along there, myself," said Muriel Phelps, anxious to be included in the conversation. "That canal goes past the back of the prisoner of war camp and some new buildings they've just put up; a strange-looking place, surrounded by high banks of soil and a forest of barbed wire security fence. I got the impression they don't want anyone to see what's going on there. It's a frightful shame that they've made such a mess in those lovely fields. There are bulldozers and diggers all over the place."

Roger Jones smiled at Miss Phelps' observation. "You can hardly be surprised about that, Muriel. This area's a hotbed of army activity and there's so much here which we probably shouldn't know about."

Mr Gloyne, disappointed with these intrusions, thought Dawn needed a prompt. "Well, Dawn. Tell us about this adventure of yours."

Everyone waited until Dawn finally swallowed her mouthful of pie.

"Well, we crossed over the canal at the humpback bridge, and past the gun emplacement there. We had a few problems with the soldiers. You know. The usual wolf whistles and invitations to inspect their pill box!"

Miss Clarke made disproving tutting sounds before adding, "What is the world coming to?"

"Where was I? Oh, yes. We were able to get down onto the towpath and we had been jogging along for only a few minutes when suddenly, out of absolutely nowhere, a group of about six planes flew really low, right over our heads. They were so low that we could clearly see the faces of the pilots as well as the rear gunners. The noise of their engines was deafening and the air was filled with their stinking exhaust fumes. It all happened so suddenly that some of the girls were quite frightened and started blubbing."

Miss Phelps gasped. "What a dreadful shock for you all! I hope the girls are none the worse from their experience?"

Eric Gloyne was less interested in the welfare of the pupils and wanted more details about the planes.

"Were they our planes or American?"

"Oh, they were American, all right. We could see the white star on their sides. And they had lots of guns poking out of them. They were so low that they barely seemed to clear the hedges!"

"I think they were probably up from Keevil," commented Colin Sharples who, up to that point, had been an attentive member of Dawn's audience. "A chap at The Crown works for a contractor," he explained, "and they've been building a new airstrip there. He says that the place was only half-finished when the Yanks turn up out of the blue with a squadron of bombers. He says they created merry hell when they found that their quarters weren't ready."

"When did this happen?" Richard Kymer was following the conversation very keenly.

"I think they've been building since last year and they'd finished the runways and perimeter track in

September. But the Yanks arrived three weeks ago, with the hangers and mess huts still half-finished. Now, they're using all the daylight hours that God sends, practising low-level formation flying. If you believe some of the stories going around, they sometimes come back with bits of branches stuck in them. No wonder they gave you a scare, Dawn."

"Goodness!" exclaimed Doris Clarke, "what a lot of information! I'm sure we shouldn't be discussing this so openly. As the posters say, *Careless Talk Costs Lives.*"

"Doris," Eric Gloyne chipped in, "you worry too much! That's for when you don't know who might be listening. I'm sure none of *us* is likely to be a threat to national security."

At this, everyone laughed in relief and Richard Kymer enquiringly turned to Dawn, who had used the interruption to polish off the rest of her shepherd's pie.

"I think that'd explain it, Colin. I had to calm a couple of the girls, but they recovered very quickly. But that's not the only shock we had because, soon after that, we rounded a bend in the towpath and our way was barred by three burly soldiers, all waving guns at us."

"How dreadful, Dawn! You certainly seem to have a knack of getting into scrapes," said Muriel Phelps. "What could they possibly want with you?"

Richard Kymer said, "Oh, I can think of several answers to that," he teased, giving Dawn a flashing smile.

His comment was lost on Muriel Phelps, but not on Dawn, who felt herself blushing at this pass by Richard

Kymer. Chris Edwards, too, had registered his comment and was watching and listening intently.

"Well, they were blocking off the towpath while some policemen and soldiers recovered a body from the canal. I managed to turn the girls back so they didn't see anything, but I could see that they were pulling the body of a prisoner of war out of the water. His uniform was sodden, but I could clearly make out those white patches they have to wear on their trousers and tunics. It was pretty gruesome!" She shivered at the recollection

"Poor devil!" Kymer had quickly become more serious. "Maybe he'd escaped over the wire from the POW camp and then drowned as he tried crossing the canal."

"How do we know he was drowned?" cut in Eric Gloyne. "That canal is so badly silted up that it can only be a couple of feet deep so you could just wade across," he added. "For all we know, he may have been shot while trying to escape!"

Further discussion on the demise of the POW was halted with the arrival of Hattie Perkins and Daisy, each pushing a large catering trolley. As Daisy, helped by several senior girls, collected the dirty dinner plates and placed them on the trolley, Hattie began serving out bread and butter pudding. In the interlude, Colin Sharples went round to each of the oil lamps which lit the room and made small adjustments to the wicks before giving the fire a poke and adding a log from the basket. As he stood up from his exertions, he noticed a pile of letters on the mantelpiece and reached up to collect it.

Hattie looked up and saw him make the discovery.

"Sorry, Mr Sharples. I meant to tell you. The post came very late today when everyone were out. So I thought as it'd be best to put it on the mantelpiece until you all came down to tea."

"Thank you, Hattie, that's absolutely fine," he said as he brought the letters to the table. Hattie had divided the post into two neat bundles, one of letters addressed to pupils and the other pile for the staff.

Colin Sharples gave the pupils' bundle to a senior girl to distribute. Receiving a letter was an exciting occurrence for the girls and, despite disproving glances from Muriel Phelps, there were some unsuppressed (Dr Madely would have called them "un lady-like") shrieks from the lucky ones, who eagerly tore open envelopes for news from home.

Meanwhile, Sharples personally distributed the staff letters, which included one for himself which, for the time being, he tucked beneath his side plate.

His lamp-lighting and stoking duties, together with the arrival of the pudding and the arrival of the post, all combined to make a welcome break in proceedings and, in a brighter and happier mood, pupils and staff resumed their meals, with no further reference to Dawn's ordeals.

Chris Edwards, who was sitting next to Colin Sharples, glanced down at the corner of his letter which protruded from under his side plate.

"Colin," she exclaimed, "did you cut yourself just now, when you were looking after the fire?"

"I don't think so," he replied, examining both hands. "Why do you ask?"

"Oh, it's just that there's a bloodstain on the corner of your letter."

"It can't have come from me," he said, showing her his hands. "Perhaps it was the postman." So saying, he picked up the envelope and placed it in the inside pocket of his jacket.

Two hours after tea, Dawn Crosby lay on her bed in her dressing gown. She'd enjoyed her bath – rationed to two per week – and now she reclined against her pillows, feeing radiant in the afterglow. She closed her eyes as her body felt a tingling surge and she pulled open her gown with one hand to fondle her raised nipples and firm breasts while, with her other hand, she began to stroke rhythmically between her legs.

Her growing excitement was interrupted by a light knock on her door, followed by a hoarse whisper. "It's me!"

"Come in," she called, and when the visitor had closed the door behind them, she sat up, allowing her dressing gown to fall open to reveal the beauty of her full nakedness. She gave her visitor an impish smile. "You took your time!" she chided, "I've been waiting for you."

Chapter Five

Police Constable Harper wearily pulled on his cycle clips, buttoned up his cape and wheeled his bike along the narrow passageway of the house which served as both home and village police station. Closing the side door behind him, he walked with stolid step down the garden path and, on reaching the small, white gate to the road, he propped his machine against the bare hedge and examined the switch on his dipped cycle torch.

He next checked his pockets for cuffs and truncheon, while reflecting on his extreme good fortune of being posted to Cannings. He had twice put in for a promotion but his superior, Sergeant Bridewell, made sure Harper's application never reached his inspector's "in" tray since, in Bridewell's view, Harper was not cut out for a senior rank. Instead, he'd been sent out "into the sticks" and, while Harper had, at first, been resentful about being overlooked, he now relished his deployment to a village away from the urban humdrum – and a more attractive village it was hard to imagine.

Nestling as it did beneath the folds of the Marlborough Downs, Barton Cannings came complete with its thatched cottages, ancient church, smithy, pub and shop. In fact, as he patrolled this rural idyll, it was sometimes hard to remember that this little corner of rural

England was gripped in the same bloody war that was being fought all over the world.

However, if he ever became complacent about his working environment, there were the two big and constant reminders to jolt him out of his smugness and both were located just a mile from the village.

The first of these was the new American garrison and army hospital, which sprawled over much of Cannings Hill to the west of the village.

On the face of it, the camp appeared entirely self-contained, separated from the village as it was by the busy London Road which linked Devizes to the west with Marlborough to the north. So, theoretically, the camp and its personnel should have had little impact on PC Harper or on the rest of the village community – but nothing could be further from the truth.

By some strange process of osmosis, the camp and its personnel contrived to permeate into the domestic life of the village and, for Jack Harper, this always resulted in more paperwork. Fights between villagers and Yanks outside the Crown Inn after closing, army lorries involved in collisions and "near misses" on the narrow village roads, disturbances at the dances held at the village school – they had all added spice to village life and made more work for PC Harper.

The second, unavoidable reminder was the imposing prison camp which had sprung up, almost overnight, beside the barracks on London Road and which housed German prisoners of war. The boundary fence of barbed wire, the guards and the constant floodlighting left no one on either side of this imposing fortification in any doubt of its purpose.

PC Harper still could not decide which of these establishments he disliked the most. As he'd mentioned to his wife, Rose, at least the Jerries were contained inside their compound. The Yanks seemed to turn up everywhere he looked.

And then there were the Scantons.

It was a cold and wet night and Harper glanced up from his bike towards the west, where the sky glowed and pulsed orange while, low on the horizon, searchlights criss-crossing the night sky in their probing for enemy aircraft. Bristol, it appeared, was getting another pasting. "Poor bastards!" he said aloud, and then gave thanks that Cannings was spared this same devastation.

He pulled his bike upright and was just about to lever himself into the saddle when he heard the big telephone bell ring on the side of the house.

Muttering under his breath, he turned off his lights, lent his bike against the hedge for a second time and ponderously retraced his steps to the building. He entered his small office, which was barely big enough to accommodate his large frame and his bulky utility furniture. He lowered himself into his chair to face his phone, which was in pride of place in the middle of his desk.

He lifted the earpiece off its hook, pulled the speaker unit towards him and cleared his throat before enunciating deliberately in his broad Wiltshire accent.

"Cannings police station. PC Harper speaking."

There followed the clunk of coins dropping in the call box as the connection was made.

"Is that you, Jack?" It was an agitated woman's voice which PC Harper immediately recognised. "Thank goodness I found you in! It's our Alfie. He's come home late an'..."

Jack Harper wasn't happy with first names being used on the phone on police business. Such informality could erode his authority in the village and he knew Heather Waite on the switchboard at nearby Horton was bound to be listening in for any titbits she could take with her to the Bridge Inn.

"It's *Constable Harper*, please, Mrs Barter, when we're on the phone," he said rather pompously. "Now, what's this about your Alfie?"

"Well, he's come home soaked to the skin an' he reckons he seen a plane land up at Baltic!"

"Now, calm down, Mrs Barter. Calm down. We know we have to take a pinch of salt with what your Alfie claims he's done, don't we?" Harper alluded to several previous occasions when Alfie Barter had variously reported seeing German paratroopers landing behind the church, Field Marshall Montgomery coming out of The Crown Inn and naked women dancing on the vicarage lawn.

"I know, I know," she said, "but this time 'e could be telling the truth!"

"Oh? An' what makes you think that?" asked PC Harper, a touch of scepticism creeping into his voice.

"Well, he told 'is story to 'is uncle George, an' George do know all about Alfie's previous nonsense so 'e threatened to take the strap to 'im if 'e found 'e were lyin'. Alfie were terrified an' screamed it were the truth."

"Right. So what did Alfie say he'd been up to this time?"

Mrs Barter paused to take a breath. "I'd sent Alfie to the lambing pens up beyond Baltic with a pasty for 'is dad. They've been kept real busy with the lambing this week an', what with this weather today, Mr Barter hasn't had a chance to come home for a meal since he left at six this morning."

"So what has that got to do with Alfie seeing this plane?"

"I think you'd better speak to him yerself so as he can tell you personal, like. Could you call round this evening before 'is bedtime? He'd still have it fresh in his mind."

"I'm just on my way out now. I've got to see the landlord at The Crown on some business first. But I could call in on you afterwards, if that'd be convenient?"

"Yes, please. That would be good of you, I'm sure. We'll see you later on, then."

With that, the line crackled and Mrs Barter rang off.

PC Harper hung up the earpiece on its hook and, donning his helmet again, he left his office and mounted his bike for the short journey to the pub.

He didn't like The Crown much. The landlord had free range chickens which often wandered into the building and the landlord had to wash the quarry tiles to remove any evidence of their visits. As a result, the place reeked strongly of a mixture of beer and disinfectant. Added to which, to PC Harper's mind, the place always seemed cold.

The wet weather had deterred many of the regular drinkers from venturing out that night although Harper was surprised to notice some customers had nevertheless braved the elements. In the bar were a couple of soldiers, two teachers from Lynton House and Stan Stagg and his brother, who were chatting to Frank Tonks. There were also two Scantons, although Harper could never tell whether they were brothers or cousins, who were enjoying a chat with two Land Army girls.

Landlord, Melvin Carter, was trying to revive a smouldering fire in the snug bar when PC Harper walked in and Carter brushed off his grubby hands on the seat of his trousers before he invited the constable through to the kitchen.

Seated at the kitchen table, Harper checked through the licensing papers which Carter had ready for the constable's visit and, when Harper found everything in order, he made ready to leave.

"Not the sort of night to be out in, Jack. If I had your job, I'd be finding a nice sheltered spot to keep out of the weather. I don't reckon as you'll be catching many criminals tonight 'cos they'll all be indoors in the warm and dry!"

"Well, it so happens I've only got one more call to make and then I will be getting home, myself. But first, I've got to look in on the Barters to follow up on the latest of young Alfie's wild stories. Reckons he saw a plane land up near Baltic, but you know how he imagines things. His mum is convinced that, this time, he could be telling the truth but I'm sure there'll be nothing in it. Any road, I've promised Mrs Barter I'd call in to hear what 'e's got to say."

With that, Harper wished Carter good night and, nodding a greeting to the drinkers in the bar, he left the odour of Jeye's Fluid behind him and escaped to the fresh air outside.

A few minutes later, a shadowy figure slipped out of the pub and started off in the direction taken by the policeman.

PC Harper leant his bike against the Barters' cottage wall beneath a window, turned off his lights and gave the door a rap.

Mrs Barter had been waiting impatiently ever since she'd returned from the phone kiosk and so, when PC Harper knocked on the door, it was wrenched open before he'd a chance to lower his hand.

"Come in, Jack, come in," she invited, "and take off your cape." He stooped to enter the low doorway from the road and she took the dripping garment from him and Harper removed his helmet. She closed the door and ushered him down the short passage to the parlour where her brother, George, sat at the table, finishing off his supper.

The small room was modestly furnished, but scrupulously clean and, sitting on the faded settee was Alfie Barter, who looked both excited and nervously apprehensive all at the same time.

At twelve years of age, Alfie was the Barters' youngest son. His much older brothers, Seth and Henry, excluded him from most of their activities and interests and so he spent much of his time on his own, without the company or friendship of other children.

Alfie was seen by headmaster, Barry Dyke, as probably one his greater challenges in terms of achieving academic prowess. However, it seems that this was compensated to a degree by his possessing an extremely fertile imagination and, in recent years, he had earned a reputation in the village of producing "stories".

As something of a "loner", he found it was a good way of getting attention from people who might otherwise have ignored his very presence and, in Alfie's jumbled-up thinking, he saw little distinction between creating stories and telling out-and-out lies.

So, it was with some caution that PC Harper felt he should investigate what Alfie had told his mother. He nodded a greeting at George.

"Alfie, this is Constable Harper," said Mr Barter, unnecessarily. "Now I want you to tell him exactly what you told me about what you seen up at Baltic."

Alfie looked relieved at the prospect of talking to someone who might listen to his account, although he flicked wary glances over Harper's shoulder towards George, who had remained at the table and who was now showing great interest in the proceedings.

Harper sank into a battered armchair opposite Alfie and took out his notebook and pencil. "Now then, Alfie, I want you to think back to this afternoon and tell me everything you remember. Take your time, now, and be sure you leave nothing out. It's important, you see, that I have all the details. To start with, why did you go up to Baltic?"

"Oh, that's easy. I took our dad a pasty for 'is tea. So I cycled up the Hollow and along London road to Baltic to give it to 'im."

"Were you on your own?" asked Harper.

"Yes."

"And when you got to the lambing pens, what did you do?"

"Well, I looked for our dad. It were rainin' 'ard an' I knew he'd be in 'is hut 'cos I could see smoke coming from the chimney. He always goes into the shepherds' hut if weather's bad. There was no lambs due for a while so him an' Cyril was sheltering there."

"How long did you stay with your father in the hut?"

"I reckon it must have been about half an hour. It must have been that long because it were starting to get dark an' our Dad had to light the hurricane lamp."

"And is that when you left the hut to come home?" Harper found he was taking Alfie's account more seriously than he had originally expected.

"Yes. I didn't want to have to cycle back in the dark because it's dangerous with all the convoys of army lorries using that road. A woman got knocked off her bike near there and were killed last week an' our mum warned me about cycling in the blackout."

"That's very sensible advice," said Harper to Alfie, glancing across at Mrs Barter, who preened with pleasure at the compliment. "So you left the pens. What happened next?"

"Well, I walked along the track from the pens to the road. The track there is a bit too rough to ride, see, so I were pushing my bike. An', just as I reached the road, I hears this strange sound. It were a sort of whooshing and whining sound. An' then, very sudden like, this plane came out of nowhere! Right over my 'ead. It were very low! It fair frightened me!"

"What sort of plane was it, Alfie?" Harper asked, pausing from his note-taking.

"Oh, I don't know what plane it were, Mr Harper."

"Well, could you see how many engines it had?"

"Yes, I could see that, all right. It had just the one, but it didn't seem to be working too good when it went over me."

"What about its wings," probed Harper, "did it have one wing or two wings?"

"Oh, it had just one wing... on top of the cabin, not like a Spitfire 'cos a Spitfire's wing is underneath the cockpit. I knows that from the charts at school," he added, proudly.

"Was the plane coloured at all? Did it have any markings that you could see?"

"Well, it's funny you should ask that because, although I only seen it for a couple of seconds when it were close up, I remember thinking that all the planes we see got circles on them – or stars, if they are a Yank. This one had nothing, not even camouflage. It just looked black."

Jack Harper made some more notes, aware he was becoming excited with Alfie's account, as it developed.

"What direction do you think it came from, Alfie?"

Alfie paused and frowned with the effort of concentration.

"It seemed to have come Beckhampton way... or it could have come from the Cherhill direction. It all happened too quick for me to be sure. But, when it went over my head, it were crossing over the road and, at first, I thought it were heading on towards Cannings Hill."

"But you don't think it did?" asked Harper.

"No, I *know* it didn't," answered Alfie, somewhat triumphantly, "'cos I saw 'im turn and drop down low. He were heading for the black barns near the Wansdyke," referring to the ancient ditch which straddled the landscape there.

Harper's voice was tense. "Did you see it land, Alfie?"

Alfie couldn't disguise the disappointment in his voice. "No, 'e vanished into the rain and then my view was blocked by Yank lorries in a slow convoy."

"Well, now, Alfie, that's been very helpful and I'm glad you remembered everything so clearly," said PC Harper, folding his notebook and getting to his feet and, from his patronising tone, he clearly implied he'd been brought out on a fool's errand.

"But that's not everything!" protested Alfie. "Later, I saw it again on the ground!"

"Are you sure about this, Alfie? You're not making this up just to please me?"

"No! Honest!"

Harper had resumed his seat and leant forward with his notebook once more at the ready. "So how did you get to see it again?"

"Well, I guessed it were heading towards the black barns further up the road at Shepherds Shore and I knew I had to get there quickly if I wanted to see it again. I knew I couldn't cycle there fast enough so," he paused, then added guiltily in a low voice, "I got a tow from the tailboard of the last lorry in the convoy!"

At this revelation, Mrs Barter jumped up from her chair. "Alfie! I've told you before that's a very dangerous thing to do. I don't care that other boys do it! What will the constable think of us?"

She made to cuff Alfie, but Harper leant forward and intervened. "What your mother says is quite right and you shouldn't do it, Alfie. But, on this occasion, I won't take any action about it. Just carry on and tell me what you saw."

Alfie's account was interrupted at this point by a loud scraping sound on the wall outside, followed by a crash. George Barter got up wearily from the table and went out to investigate. There were some more scraping sounds and thuds and George returned a few minutes later, flicking rain off his head and arms.

"S'all right, Jack. 'T wer your bike. Either you 'adn't parked 'im proper, or else someone must've walk into 'im. I've put 'im agin the house so 'e won't fall over agin."

PC Harper was puzzled by this but thanked Baker for his kindness. He was sure the bike wouldn't have fallen on its own. He then looked expectantly again towards Alfie, who was annoyed by the interruption to his account.

"Carry on, Alfie."

"Right. There was lots of spray from the lorry and I don't think the driver could see me. When we was level with the track that leads to the barns, I let go the tailboard and freewheeled off the road into the gateway. That's when I saw the plane again – on the ground! Leastways, I saw the back half of it sticking out beyond the buildings." Alfie's face was aglow with excitement as he re-lived his experience.

"What happened next?" asked Harper, who was busy making jottings in his notebook.

"I wanted to have a closer look 'cos I ain't seen a plane on the ground up close. So I thought I'd creep over towards the barn. But then two things happened suddenly what gave me a fright."

"And what were they?" By this stage of Alfie's narrative, Harper, George and Mrs Barter were all leaning forward in intense concentration.

"Well, the first thing was the engine of the plane gave a sudden loud revving sound and it jumped forward so as I couldn't see it any more. I think it went right into the barn. I was still crouching by the gateway and I knew I had to get closer if I were going to see anything. But, just when I was going to head up the track, I seen a man."

"Where had he come from?" Harper was no longer writing, he was so absorbed with Alfie's account.

"I think he'd been sheltering in the hedge further up the track. He didn't see me 'cos he were looking towards the barn, too, and it were raining hard. But I thought he acted strange, like, 'cos he bent down low and ran all doubled up – as though he didn't want anyone to see him."

"Where did he run to, Alfie?"

"Towards the sheds by the barn but, by then, it was getting dark and I couldn't see him against the buildings. He had on this dark rain coat and it was difficult to see him."

"So what did you do then?"

"Well, I waited for a bit because I thought that, if the pilot left the barn, I could creep and look inside. But I didn't want the other man to know I'd seen him, either. Then a big black car came out from the barn. That was a surprise, because I didn't know it was there. Its lights weren't on and it came right towards me down the track, so I had to hide back in the hedge, quick. I could see some people in the car as it passed me but it were difficult to tell how many they was. Then two blokes walked from the barn down the track towards me. I was sure they'd see me, but they walked on past where I were hiding. That was frightening, I can tell you!"

Alfie's audience was totally engrossed in his account of his adventure and they looked expectantly towards him for more.

"By this time, I were getting soaked and I thought I'd go back for my bike and come home. But, just then, the man I seen before left the barns and came walking over the field towards me. He caught his coat on the wire fence when he climbed over it and then he walked past me, back towards the road."

"Could you describe this man, Alfie? Would you know him again if you saw him?"

"I'm not too sure. It were so dark, Mr Harper. I couldn't see his face from where I were tucked into the hedge. In any case he'd pulled his hat down over it. But I'll tell you one thing! His coat had sort of buckles on his sleeves. And I'll tell you something else, too. Whoever it was, he'll have nice rip in his raincoat!"

PC Harper made some notes before asking Alfie to continue.

"Did you get a look in the barn, Alfie?"

"What do *you* think? I'd been waiting long enough! Yes, I ran up the track and round to the front. I had a look in one of the windows but I couldn't see anything inside 'cos it were pitch black. The strange thing was that I had seen the plane there with my own eyes – but now, there was nothing to see. Nothing! The place looked like it were never used. The one thing I can remember, though, was this strong smell, like petrol."

"So, that's when you decided you'd better come home?"

"Yes," he replied in a disappointed tone and, turning to Mrs Baker, added, "and I'm sorry, our mum, for getting so wet – an' I promise I won't get any more tows from lorries!"

PC Harper stood up and carefully placed his notebook in the breast pocket of his uniform and secured the flap with its shining button.

"Now listen to me, Alfie. What you've told me could be very important. So, for the time being, I want you to promise that you say nothing to anyone else about this. Do you understand? And the same goes for you two," he said, turning to Mrs Barter and George. "Not a word!" They all nodded their agreement and PC Harper bade them goodnight and left them to return to the station through the drizzle – the same drizzle which obscured from his view a figure, lurking in the bushes opposite the cottage.

PC Harper had spent much of the previous evening writing up his report and he had debated on whether to hand it straight in to Sergeant Bridewell but, in the end, decided that he'd pay a visit to Baltic first, to check out Alfie's story.

Although the rain had lifted, there was a keen easterly wind blowing across the downs as Harper climbed breathlessly to the top of the Hollow and turned onto London Road, towards Beckhampton. The headwind made for hard pedalling and it took some ten minutes before he reached the barns at Shepherd's Shore.

He dismounted and stood in the entrance to the track that Alfie had described and took in the scene; the track and the hedgerow under which Alfie had hidden, the black barns and the outbuildings and the intervening field and wire fence over which Alfie had seen the man climb.

He listened intently for any sound of activity but heard nothing except for the constant humming of the wind in the overhead telephone wires and the equally constant cry from a flock of lapwings in an adjacent ploughed field.

Harper lifted his bike into the hedge and ventured up the track on foot, pausing occasionally to listen, but he heard nothing. Emboldened, he set out more purposefully and, a few minutes later, he had reached the barn with its outbuildings.

The entrance to the barn was on the side furthest from the road, which tied in with Alfie's account, and here he stopped again and listened. There was nothing but the cry of lapwings and the drone of a passing formation of planes overhead. So he approached the window through which Alfie had looked and peered in under the shade of his raised hand.

The grime on the window prevented a clear view, and it was only possible to make out a number of dark shapes inside which resembled piles of straw bales. There was certainly no obvious or recognisable shape of an aircraft and he was just beginning to wonder if Alfie's account was, after all, a concoction of his imagination when he noticed an unusual smell. It was the pungent smell which wafted in the wind from an area of ground in front of the main barn doors. He stooped and, with finger and thumb, picked up a small sample of soil and held it to his nose. The smell was intense and unmistakable. It was definitely that of high octane aviation fuel! So Alfie hadn't been imagining this, after all.

From his stooped position, Harper looked around him for any other telltale signs which might indicate the barn had been used recently. There were certainly no wheel tracks but he knew they could easily have been brushed away or covered over.

Then he looked more closely at the large barn doors, which were suspended from a continuous tracking high above his head. And he gave a start for, while at a casual glance the building gave the appearance of neglect and disuse, the underside of the tracking and the rollers on the doors glistened with freshly applied grease! "Bugger me!" he said under his breath. "So Alfie *was* right!"

These discoveries set Harper's mind buzzing. His first thought was to force an entry to look inside the barn but, on reflection, he decided against this because he could leave evidence of his visit which might scare away his quarry – whoever they might be. In any event, despite its dilapidated appearance, the barn was still sufficiently sturdy to deny any scope for a break-in.

So Harper stood up and looked around the other outbuildings, but found nothing of interest.

His next thought concerned the car and its occupants and where they could have been taken. He was aware that a strange car in the neighbourhood would be very conspicuous – mainly because there were so few cars on the road due to petrol rationing – and those people that ran a car were already well-known to the authorities. So it seemed unlikely that this car could have travelled to

Devizes or to Swindon without exciting attention – something that these people apparently wanted to avoid. Certainly, if such a car had turned up in Barton Cannings, he'd have heard about it very quickly from his own information network; the same would certainly be true for any of the other local villages.

So perhaps, he reasoned, this vehicle was used for much shorter journeys. He walked around the barn to the track and looked about him. What he saw was mile after mile of open, rolling downland, with the only buildings visible being those across on the other side of the road, clustered inside a windbreak of beech trees at Baltic Farm, about a mile away.

PC Harper thought he should at least eliminate the farm from his enquiries while he was there and so he retraced his steps, mounted his bike and headed along the road to the turning up to the farm and turned in to the entrance.

The track way entered a tunnel of beech trees and he had only pedalled twenty yards towards the farm when he heard someone shout, "Stop!" The next moment, two soldiers, wearing the insignia of the military police and brandishing Sten guns, ran out from behind a tree and barred his way.

Harper skidded to a halt, his heart racing.

"Here! What's going on?" he demanded, desperately trying to maintain an air of authority. "I'm Police Constable Harper, and this farm is on my patch. What are you blokes doing here?"

The senior soldier, a sergeant, stepped forward, careful to keep out of his colleague's line of fire.

"Sorry mate. This is a restricted area under the terms of the War Act and I've got to ask you to turn round and leave!"

"But I need to make some enquiries at the farm in connection with a police investigation," he retorted pompously, unwilling to back down. "So I have every right to go up this road!"

"Every right, my arse! I don't care if you're bloody Winston Churchill, mate. No one's allowed beyond this point. Now let's be turning round and clearing off!"

Harper noticed that, throughout this exchange, the muzzles of the Sten guns pointed unwaveringly at him but he still didn't move. "I'll be reporting this incident to my superiors. You men could find yourselves in serious trouble!"

At this point both soldiers flipped off the safety catches of their weapons and took a pace forwards, their weapons extended ready to fire.

That was sufficient for Harper, who turned his bike round and cycled down the track as fast as his heavy legs would take him. When he glanced back over his shoulder, the two were still standing in the same menacing pose until Harper turned onto the main road and they were lost from sight.

Back at the police station he made a telephone call to Devizes.

"Hello, this is Police Constable Jack Harper, number 562, at Barton Cannings. I need to speak urgently with Sergeant Bridewell!"

Chapter Six

Ali pushed her bike up the last fifty yards of the Hollow, which sloped steeply up from the crossroads in the village. Despite her extra, warm clothing and vigorous exercise in reaching the top of the hill, she was still aware of the cold as the wind cut across the exposed hillside.

She checked her watch and saw she still had ten minutes to wait before the appointed *rendezvous*. She pulled her bike off the road and hid it in the ditch and walked up the last few yards to the crossroads.

London Road, which mercifully bypassed Barton Cannings, was a major route connecting Bristol in the west with the capital and, even in peacetime, it carried a heavy volume of mainly commercial traffic. However, since the outbreak of war, it had now become even busier, due partly to the increased transport of goods associated with the War effort and also because of the addition of military vehicles. The deafening noise was unrelenting and, as Ali waited, a convoy of large army trucks crawled past, their heavy duty tyres making a characteristic throbbing as the vehicles headed towards Devizes. The cabs on many of the vehicles were open to the elements and the drivers huddled down against the cold, swathed in extra layers of clothing and peering ahead through their goggles.

Going in the opposite direction were large commercial lorries, some hauling equally large trailers. They were heavily overloaded and the straining engines belched out volumes of blue smoke which was quickly dispersed on the strong wind. The vehicles' blackout headlights gave only a feeble beam by which to drive, and Ali realised she'd have to keep a sharp lookout if she was to see the car she was due to meet.

She checked her watch again, her hands trembling as much from excitement as from the cold. By the lights from the passing vehicles she could just make out that she still had five minutes to wait. Then, just as she was beginning to wonder if she'd misunderstood her directions, a large, black saloon pulled in from behind a column of lorries and stopped in the small lay-by beside her.

The driver, a man wearing a high-collared Macintosh coat and a trilby hat, leant over to open the passenger door.

He yelled out above the din, "Good evening, miss. D'you have a password for me?"

"Oh, yes. Roundway," she yelled back.

"Right, miss. Hop in!"

"Thank you," said Ali, and she slid gratefully into the front seat, a sanctuary from the noise and cold. Inside, the car was warm, with a pervading smell of petrol.

As they moved out into the traffic, she looked sideways at the driver, who resembled someone from a Hollywood gangster film she'd seen at the Palace cinema in Devizes, and she suddenly felt extremely vulnerable.

"Can you tell me where we're going?" She tried to conceal the anxiety she was now feeling.

"Sorry, miss, I can't tell you," he replied. Was that a smirk she could see on his face?

"Then at least tell me who I'm going to meet."

"I can't tell you that, either, miss. My instructions was to collect you and deliver you."

"But surely you can say where we are heading!" she exclaimed.

The driver kept his eyes to the front, concentrating on the road, and said nothing.

In the silence that followed Ali thought she should concentrate on her surroundings. The trappings inside of the car, for a start, indicated that this had, in its day, been a rather expensive vehicle. The dash was polished wood, with chromed dials and switches. From the door pillars there hung intricately tasselled silk grab ropes and covering the floor was a deep carpet. Glancing down, Ali saw that, beneath the dash, a shelf, also finished in shining wood, extended across the width of the vehicle. A courtesy light glowed softly above it, sufficient to reveal gloves and a folded newspaper. Then her heart gave a jolt when she realised that, poking out from the newspaper, was the butt of a gun. She felt it would be best not to acknowledge that she'd seen the weapon and she fixed her gaze on the shapes of the passing landscape.

With a number of grating gear changes, the car reluctantly climbed Cannings Hill before dropping down towards the army camp. In the gloom and to her right, she could see the outline of huts on the edge of the American hospital and, soon after, they were passing the imposing silhouette of Le Marchant Barracks.

"At least I know where we are, so far," she thought, and this was then confirmed by the pungent smell of retting from the flax factory, which increased in strength as they drew closer to it.

The complete blackout conditions meant that Ali had only outline shapes of buildings for her navigation of the route and she was just congratulating herself on her success at recognising her whereabouts when, without ceremony or warning, the vehicle abruptly turned right between two large pillars and past a squat lodge and the journey was plunged into total darkness, as the car proceeded cautiously along a drive under a dense canopy provided by an avenue of trees.

This was new territory to her and so she focussed hard on the way ahead, although this was made difficult by the poor illumination from the car's headlights and the characterless nature of the route – a long, straight, tarmac driveway bordered by evenly planted conifers.

After a mile, the car lights picked up a security barrier, manned by two armed guards, who waved the driver to stop. While they waited, Ali noticed that there were a number of troops in under the deep cover provided by the trees. There was a brief check of papers, followed by a torch being shone in her face, and then they were on their way again.

After a further period of some five minutes, during which the driver made no attempt at any conversation, the trees fell away and the roadway broadened out abruptly onto a wide expanse of gravel in front of a large building. In the dark, it was difficult for Ali to see it clearly, but the dipped headlights picked up the faced stone of what appeared to be a significant property. The large casement windows on the ground floor were blanked by shutters and were surrounded by ornate stonework. Looking up, Ali got the impression of walls extending up high above her, punctuated with many more windows and topped by castellation, silhouetted against the night sky. This was, indeed, a country mansion of some standing. To confirm this, the impressive entrance comprised double front doors, set between pillars which supported a large stone canopy. And standing in the shadows cast by the porch she could see a man, guarding the entrance.

The driver turned the car on the gravel to bring it to rest beside the steps to the entrance.

"End of the road, miss. This is where you get out. You're to report to the security guard."

"A man of many words," thought Ali, as she slid out of the car and walked towards the imposing entrance. The car, meanwhile, pulled away and disappeared around the side of the building.

"Good evening. I'm here for a meeting…"

"Been expecting you, miss. Please follow me!" The guard opened one of the heavy front doors, pulled aside the blackout curtain and motioned for her to enter. "Please go through the inner door. Someone will be waiting for you." She heard him replace the blackout curtain and the heavy door closed noisily behind her.

Ali walked across the matting of the large entrance porch to glazed, double doors. She pulled on one of the large brass handles to find herself in a gloomy and spacious, wood-panelled hallway, off which there were a number of large doors. The floor was chequered in black and white marble and, overhead, hung a large, dusty electric chandelier with many of its bulbs missing and so providing limited light.

Clearly, the mansion had seen better days and a mustiness hung in the air. Ahead of her, on the far side of the hall, a grand staircase led upwards and, from the landing above, swags of new communications cables hung down in brightly coloured bundles which, on reaching the floor, snaked across it to disappear under some of the doors.

Groups of chairs clustered against the wall beside some of the doors, which reminded her a bit of a dentist's waiting room. Standing in one of the doorways was a well-built, armed guard, who immediately called across to her.

"Come and take a seat, miss," he called out, indicating the chairs beside him. "The Controller will see you in a moment."

She noted that still no names were mentioned, and that the guards, like the driver, wore no uniforms but they were all armed.

"Thank you," she said and made her way over and took a seat.

Occasionally, the door to one of the rooms would open, accompanied by the loud sound of chattering typewriters, and a civilian clerk would come out, carrying bundles of papers, and would clatter across the echoing hall to disappear into another room. A uniformed guard, restraining a panting Alsatian dog, came in the front door and walked past her before turning the corner, to vanish down another echoing corridor. Throughout, the guard beside her made no attempt to speak to her but stood, motionless, in the doorway.

Eventually, the handle rattled preparatory to the door opening and the guard immediately turned and entered the room, from which came the sounds of conversation. There was a pause while he spoke in low tones with someone and then he returned.

"The Controller will see you now, miss. Please go in."

During her wait, Ali had started to feel more relaxed in her new surroundings but, with the abrupt summons, her apprehension returned. She stood and walked into the room, wondering what to expect.

Inside, there stretched a large, polished table beneath a bright, central light. The table took up much of the floor space and seated around it were seven people, five in civilian dress and two high-ranking, uniformed officers – one, a soldier and one, a policeman. Each person had papers spread out in front of them. In her initial glance around her, she registered that over the faded wallpaper were hanging various maps, some of Wiltshire while others were of southern England and one of Europe.

"Welcome, Miss Jenkins. I'm glad you were able to be with us this evening. Please come in and join us." This was from the man with a mop of grey hair and who was reclining almost nonchalantly at the head of the table and wearing a brown, long-sleeved pullover with elbow patches, and buttoned down the front.

Despite his appearance, he immediately gave Ali the feeling that his relaxed demeanour belied an air of authority – probably ex-army and probably a senior rank. His drawling welcome was strangely casual and informal, almost as though Ali had been invited to join his exclusive club rather than a covert, wartime operation. Yet, at the same time, she detected a steely edge to his cultured accent.

He waved her to a vacant, leather upholstered chair at the table and paused while she settled into her seat.

He continued. "Miss Jenkins. Be clear on your understanding. What you hear this evening is highly classified and goes no further than this room. I remind you that you have signed the Official Secrets Acts of 1920 and 1939 by which you are bound." There was a pause and he tilted his head forward and looked over his half glasses at Ali, rather like a benign headmaster, and she felt obliged to reply.

"I understand, sir."

"Normally, as an operative of the GHQ Auxiliary, I would not ask you to reveal the existence of the movement in which you serve to anyone, or your identity. However, we find ourselves in exceptional circumstances which call for exceptional measures and so I have taken the unprecedented step of asking you to join us this evening for a rather special briefing. During the course of the meeting I shall introduce you to the people you see sitting round the table as this becomes necessary."

He paused, scratching his head as he mulled over a point, before continuing. "But, first of all, tell me if you've ever heard of RDF."

"No, I'm afraid I haven't, sir," she answered.

"Then perhaps I could ask Dr Jarvis, here, to give us all a reminder of what RDF is all about." He turned to the middle-aged man on his right. "Dr Jarvis?"

"Thank you, Controller. RDF. is the acronym for *Radio Direction Finder*. Simply put, it's a device to detect the whereabouts of aircraft before we can physically see them. We've been developing this for a couple of years now, in conjunction with our American colleagues. But the project stalled when the Americans decided to go down a different route using a phonics system. However, we continued in the belief that the preferred system should be visual and I'm pleased to report that we've made a real breakthrough with this principle at our new premises near the POW camp, which we shall refer to as Horton Lab. Top secret, of course and, if the system works, as we believe it will, it could have a major impact on the War. It would, for example, alert anti-aircraft gunners and shipping to the approach of enemy aircraft and pilots would be able to detect hostile aircraft in the dark in order to intercept them!"

Dr Jarvis paused to let his information be absorbed by his lay audience, which made various noises of surprise and incredulity and the Controller used this break to cut in.

"Thank you Dr Jones. It is, indeed, a remarkable advance in technical science and one which we intend to guard carefully." He looked round the table, before continuing. "There is, however, a fly in the ointment. We know that we've had a breach of security. Two nights ago, an intruder at the Horton Lab was caught on the premises trying to escape through the wire. He was wearing black POW overalls – presumably to avoid detection in the dark. When he was challenged by the security guards, he tried to make a break for it and was shot as he tried to cross the canal. This incident raises three important questions to which we currently have no answers."

The Controller looked at his audience.

"The first concerns the man we caught – who was he? We know nothing about him, who he was, his nationality, nothing! Secondly, we don't know what information he may have learned or passed on about our breakthrough on RDF. And thirdly, we need to ask how anyone knew about the work going on in that site in the first place. "

At this point, the Controller turned to a much younger man at the table, dressed in a dark suit. Handsome, and in his early thirties, his slick, dark hair contrasted with the Controller's tousled, unruly grey mop.

"Commander Pritchard, would you please brief us on the MI5 perspective?"

Pritchard leant forward on his elbows, hands clasped, and surveyed the occupants of the room.

"Certainly, Controller." He cleared his throat and regarded his colleagues. "But, before I talk about the specifics confronting us here, it may be helpful to the meeting if I gave a general overview of the progress made by MI5 in counter-intelligence since the War started."

The assenting nods around the table gave him the go-ahead he'd hoped for.

"I should explain that the presence of German agents in Britain hadn't come as a complete surprise to us. We knew at the outbreak of the War that Germany had recruited quite a large network of spies up and down the country. Fortunately for us, most were poorly trained and equipped and so they were easily detected and, as a result, we've been able to mop up most of them – although a few slipped through the net. What's more, we've been very successful in getting those we caught to work for us. What we call in the trade, 'turning' them. So, many are now double agents working for British interests."

He looked round room to check his 'class' was keeping up with him.

"What we do is give them information to pass to their spy masters in Germany – information which is accurate but which has no importance… or information which, when added to other snippets from other sources, creates a plausible yet completely misleading picture. This deception has been most successful, partly because it's information that the German High Command is expecting to hear. Sometimes the information *is* both accurate *and* strategically important but, in these cases, we make sure that the information arrives just too late to have any value to the enemy! This serves to enhance an agent's credibility in the eyes of the German spy masters, who are thrilled that their agents are so well placed to provide them with such accurate information."

Pritchard turned to the Controller.

"I'm sorry for what must have sounded like a mini-lecture, Controller, but I think it will help everyone's understanding on our present position."

The Controller waved a dismissive hand.

"Absolutely, Commander. Pray, continue."

"Now, if I can refer to MI5 interests in this neighbourhood. The intelligence community has been aware in recent weeks of an increase in clandestine radio traffic in southern England, but it has only recently been able to confirm that the centre for this activity is here, right in this area." He looked round the table.

"We now have a number of our people in place, keeping an eye on some individuals we suspect of spying and we believe that at least one of these is linked to the security breach at Horton Lab."

Pritchard gauged from the raised eyebrows around the table that some members found this disturbing news.

"However, I should explain," resumed Pritchard, "that this is not our sole interest in this neck of the woods. You see, there are several other reasons why enemy agents are likely to be snooping around here. First, there is the POW camp. We suspect that some internees could well have information which might be valuable to the enemy, if only they could contact someone on the outside. But it's military intelligence which has greatest importance and is our particular concern. You will doubtless be aware of the increased military activity in the area. It's large-scale and almost impossible to conceal and it's all in preparation for a joint exercise, involving allied troops, which could swing the War back in our favour. However, I'm not at liberty to go into any further detail on that at this stage."

At this point, Ali raised a hand, looking to the Controller.

"Yes, Miss Jenkins?"

"Can I ask Commander Pritchard a question, please, Controller?"

"Please fire away. After hearing this, I'm sure it's raised some questions a number of us would like answers to."

"Thank you," said Ali, then she looked across at Pritchard. "Commander Pritchard, you explained just now that we have German double agents working for British intelligence. How do these people operate?"

Pritchard seemed to have been anticipating the query from the meeting and he gave her a smile.

"It's a good question, Miss Jenkins. I should have explained that they are made up of ordinary, English-speaking people who engaged in this work either on idealistic grounds or because they were lured by greed. The German spy masters paid well, you see. However, faced with alternative of execution for their treachery or accepting payment from the British Government, they chose to work for us."

"Yes, I see that. But what do they actually *do*?"

"Well, they had already become immersed in the community before War came along, doing ordinary jobs. They clearly needed to keep inconspicuous and to blend in with their surroundings and the same still applies. They would have little value and would be unlikely to survive if they attracted attention. So most of our double agents are engaged in everyday trades and professions and you'd pass them in the street, unnoticed. Their spying activities usually involve picking up scraps of information which they think could be woven into a deceptive story to send back to Germany and they are mentored at regular briefings with their controllers."

A balding man with a florid complexion and sporting a tweed jacket leant forward in his chair and introduced himself.

"Commander Pritchard, I'm Colonel Bridges. You've explained to us about the success MI5 has had in getting German agents to work for us but you haven't told us about the ones you referred to as slipping through your net. Are we to understand these are still at large and, if so, shouldn't we be trying to catch the blighters?"

"Thank you, Colonel. You raise an important point there. I *can* tell you that we know the whereabouts of most of these and our policy now is to keep an eye on them, rather than to attempt to arrest them. We can then try to penetrate their network using our double agents and find out more about their intentions. We're able to do this because agents rarely, if ever, meet with other spies and they don't know each other's identities. I'm pleased to say that this 'softly, softly' strategy has proved successful in most cases, but with the exception of the unfortunate incident at Horton Lab."

Colonel Bridges flicked glances between the Controller and the Commander and, by the tone of his muttered thanks, he showed he was not wholly satisfied with the answer he'd been given.

"Now, Controller, to return to the specifics in the county, there is another reason why this is a sensitive area which will be of interest to German intelligence and, with your permission, Controller, I'll ask Rosemary Masters to explain."

He turned to an attractive, blonde woman sitting across the table from him. At any other time she would have been bright and vivacious but, on this evening, her face was pale and drawn and her bandaged hand was clearly giving her pain.

"Thank you, Commander. As you heard, my name is Rosemary Masters and I'm a captain in Military Intelligence, seconded to SOE. I'm involved with counter-intelligence and my job is to train men and women to go behind enemy lines with the purpose of gathering intelligence and disrupting the German war effort. The work that these people do is extremely dangerous and the young people who volunteer for it know they are putting their lives at risk. They are particularly talented, and I need hardly add they're extremely courageous."

The Controller pushed back his grey hair, looked over the top of his glasses and asked, "Can you please explain for us where this training takes place, Captain?"

"I'm afraid I can't go into too much detail on the locations, Controller, except to tell you that there are several places in southern England where these people are prepared for their work."

At this point, she stood and went to the county map, which was hanging behind her.

"However, I *can* disclose that the one particular site I'm involved with makes use of a remote farm on the Marlborough Downs, just north of Devizes at a place known locally as Baltic." She pointed to the relevant areas as she spoke.

"It's ideally suited because the farm there and its outbuildings are remote from the nearest habitation and well screened from view by a plantation of trees. It has all the facilities I need for theory work and practical training and it's conveniently close to a small, grass airstrip which we use to transport our agents."

At this she returned to her seat.

Colonel Bridges had anticipated that a junior officer could have little to offer the meeting and, when Rosemary Masters was invited to make her contribution, he made an overt show of disinterest and shuffled his papers in front of him. After all, prior to his retirement, he'd been commanding far more senior staff and he almost resented having such a junior rank – a woman at that – being given such credence at such an important meeting.

But, when Masters referred to the Baltic training centre, he dropped his papers and turned to the Controller.

"Sir! I really do think we have to call into question the wisdom of MI6 in listening to the advice of such a junior officer on setting up shop in what is clearly an unsuitable location! Dammit, it's easily visible and hardly the most secure place to be playing their little games. Why they can't do this on Salisbury Plain and train with the soldiers who are doing the real fighting, beats me!"

For the first time since her arrival, Ali felt an uneasy atmosphere in the room. But she was surprised to see that, if the Colonel had thought his outburst would jolt the Controller out of his relaxed attitude, he was to be greatly disappointed. From his reclining position, the Controller's only response was to look across to the officer.

"Colonel, may I enquire if you know the downland to the north of Devizes?"

"Course I do – used to farm half of it myself, before the War."

"Ah! So would you say that you know the area well?"

"*Extremely* well!"

"Including the area around Baltic?"

"Yes!" Bridges' red face was beginning to get blotchy as he became tetchy with this cross-examination.

"Colonel, do you pass this place frequently?"

"Yes, several times a week."

"And how many times have you seen Captain Masters' people training there?"

There was a pause before he answered, "I haven't seen them but—"

The Controller cut in.

"Did you know that Baltic was being used for this work?"

"No! But that's not—"

Again the Controller cut in with his languid tone.

"So you know Baltic well. You haven't seen any activity at Baltic. You didn't know the use to which it was being put and you had no inkling of the whole operation. It seems to me that Captain Masters is to be congratulated on selecting such a suitable site and to have concealed its location and purpose from someone as expert in the area as you!"

The Colonel fumed, "Controller! You're missing the—"

"Colonel! Can I ask if, in all your service, you were ever wounded in action?"

"No! I wasn't. But that has no bearing—"

"Colonel, just now you implied that the work that Captain Masters and her team were engaged in – you called it *playing games* – was less exposed to danger than front line troops. Just to dispel this notion, I'd like to ask Captain Masters a few questions."

Throughout this dialogue, Masters had sat stiffly upright, only her eyes flicking to and fro between the speakers. When her name was mentioned, she turned to face the Controller.

"Captain, would you please tell the meeting where you were three days ago?"

"I was in France."

"And are you able to tell us where in France, please? I presume this won't compromise your operation in any way if you let us have this information?"

"No, not all. I was in a place called Alençon, south of Caen."

When the Controller asked his next question he was looking the Colonel in the eye.

"Alençon is in enemy hands, isn't?"

"Yes, sir."

"What was your mission, Captain?"

"Two of our operatives had been betrayed by quislings, aided, we believe, by information transmitted from this area by an enemy agent. They were being held at the Alençon Gestapo headquarters for interrogation. One of our agents was in uniform, impersonating a Gestapo officer and we knew that his prospects were particularly bleak. Our job was to get them out from there at all costs and as quickly as possible."

"Did you complete your mission successfully?"

"Only partially, I'm afraid, sir. We had the help of the Maquis to break into the stronghold and we managed to get them out OK. But the place was heavily guarded and, in the firefight which followed, one of the agents was hit and later died. But we succeeded in getting out the agent in uniform."

"I expect the Colonel and the rest of us would want to know. Who led this mission?"

"I did, sir."

"And I see from the bandage that your hand is injured. Did you sustain that during the operation?"

"Yes."

The Captain looked slightly embarrassed about her injury being the centre of attention.

The tension in the room had reached a climax and, at the conclusion of the Captain's narrative, there were sounds of people breathing out in relief, admiration and sympathy.

The Controller, who had remained leaning backwards in his chair throughout, looked pointedly across at Colonel Bridges and smiled.

"I think we are all indebted to Captain Masters in more senses than one for the splendid job she's doing," he drawled. "Clearly there are areas of her work which may be news to us and I think that none of us round this table is now under any misunderstanding regarding the dangers it involves or the qualities of leadership that are necessary for it to be successful."

There was a muted chorus of "Well done!", "Absolutely!" and "Good show!" from around the table.

The Colonel recognised the lifeline he'd been offered and he coughed, cleared his throat and blew his nose before finally saying, with stiff reluctance, "Yes! Quite so! I do concede that this work is frightfully important, Controller, and I join you in commending Captain Masters on an excellent show." Then he continued, "But I still come back to the suitability of Baltic as the location. Especially as part of the airstrip can be seen from the road and an aircraft landing or taking off there is bound to attract unwelcome attention!"

"Captain, the Colonel appears to have point. What precautions do you take to avoid the aircraft from being seen?"

"We have, indeed, addressed that possibility and we use a system which, until yesterday, had proved to be successful in avoiding detection. In the first place, flights in and out of the strip are infrequent and irregular so they follow no pattern which could be anticipated by any observer."

In view of the Colonel's persistent criticism, the Captain might have been forgiven if she'd appeared to be on the defensive; instead, she delivered her explanation in a professional, informative voice, devoid of any defensive edge.

"Secondly," she continued, "arrivals and departures are timed to coincide with first or last light. This gives our pilot the bare minimum visibility required for safety and it coincides with times when any motorists, who might be using the nearest roads, are concentrating on looking where they are going, rather than looking around them. The final precaution involves the direction of our flight path. Whenever possible, we approach the strip from the direction of Avebury in the east, which means we are coming in over the downs and so avoiding flying over any towns or villages."

"And what happens to the plane when it's not in use?"

"It's stored away in a large barn and camouflaged with straw bales and sheeting. We also take the precaution of doing some cosmetic work outside to make the building look dilapidated and unused."

At this point, Commander Pritchard intervened, looking to the Controller.

"If I can come in here, Controller. The arrangements described by Captain Masters have worked most successfully for the past nearly eighteen months. Successfully, that is, until three nights ago when, unfortunately, the plane was seen landing by the son of a local farm worker."

"How did this come about?"

"Well, sir, as you know, we've had bad weather for the past week and the return flight from France was affected by high winds and poor visibility. As a consequence, the pilot was blown off course. So, instead of the usual approach to Baltic from over Avebury, he found he was nearly over Cherhill – that's away to the west – when he needed to make his final approach. He was low on fuel by this time and light was fading fast so he had no option but take a direct course for the airstrip which, unfortunately, meant crossing the road at low altitude. It must have been at this point that the boy saw the plane."

The Controller eased himself forward in his chair before looking over to the uniformed policeman.

"Deputy Commissioner Harding, I know your people have become involved here. Would you please tell the meeting what has been the police connection."

Harding was a large, heavily built man in his late fifties and from the way in which he appeared to fill his uniform, his senior status had ensured he'd seen little active policing for some time. He was, however, good at his job, he possessed a shrewd brain and was an excellent manager of people and so he'd taken considerable interest in the way in which the Controller had just handled the Colonel's outburst.

"Thank you, Controller. Yes, our interest in the matter arose from a report a sergeant at Devizes had received from one of his constables, who's stationed at Barton Cannings. You will have seen from Captain Masters' report that Barton Cannings is the village nearest to Baltic. Evidently, a twelve-year-old boy from this village had been to see his father at the lambing pens, which are about one mile east of Baltic. This boy was close to the road, when the plane flew low over his head. Being an inquisitive youngster and knowing the area, he deduced it was heading for some local hay barns. He cycled along the road in that direction and found his assumption was correct."

DC Harding regarded with interest the various facial expressions round the table at the information he was reporting. Pritchard and Masters showed little emotion while Ali looked anxious and the Colonel appeared barely able to contain the reservations he'd voiced previously.

"He evidently witnessed the plane going into the barn and the departure of the Captain's party by car. But, more significant to the business of this meeting, he also claims to have seen someone else who had been watching. This person evidently looked around the site when everyone else had left, before leaving himself."

Harding had everyone's attention as he continued.

"When the constable later investigated the site he found it was apparently abandoned, so your efforts to camouflage your use of the barn, Captain, were most effective." Pritchard and Masters remained impassive, while Ali looked relieved.

"However, the constable did detect a strong smell of aviation spirit, which corroborated the boy's story, and this led him to check out Baltic Farm to see if there was a connection between the farm and the barn. And it was at this point," he looked to the army officer beside him, "that he was met by your men, Brigadier, who sent him packing."

The Brigadier, who had yet to speak, merely gave a faint smile and nodded.

"In conclusion, Controller, I can confirm that the constable put the fear of God into the boy and his family not to divulge this information to anyone. Similarly, my sergeant has impressed on the constable the need for confidentiality and I've every confidence that the incident has been contained in that respect. Just one other thing – we've recovered a small sample of fabric left by the mystery man when he tore his coat on the wire near the barn. This may be helpful in any later investigations. I should add," he said, looking round the table, "that it's been presumed throughout that this person is a man but it could, of course have been a woman!"

The Controller nodded to Harding.

"Thank you, Deputy Commissioner. That was most succinct. So," he continued, looking around at his colleagues, "where does that leave us? We have a possible security leak at Horton Lab where a top secret project is being developed. We believe German intelligence agents may be active in the area and some of Commander Pritchard's double agents may be involved. We have the build-up for a major, joint, military operation. Close by, we have a training base for agents destined to go behind enemy lines in Europe and, if that isn't enough, we have a sighting of an unknown person who's shown an interest in that operation!"

The Controller scratched his head as he regarded his notes in front of him, before appearing to reach a decision.

"So, this is what we do. Firstly, we need to look at those things where we hold the initiative and have control. The first of these is security, which is of paramount importance. So I want all security measures to be tightened up. If they are tight already, make them even tighter. This will obviously apply both to military and to civilian forces. Check and re-check procedures for vetting admissions to barracks and sensitive areas. Make sure all identity passes are presented and scrutinised, and not just glanced at – that includes for *everyone*, including top brass. Even if Monty turns up, I'd want his ID to be checked thoroughly. There can be no exceptions."

Everyone round the table was hurriedly jotting notes as the Controller continued, "Next, we must be even more alert and vigilant. If, in our daily routine, we see something which we haven't noticed before, make a note of it and then investigate it. It might be something trivial but, equally, it could be something major. We must avoid making presumptions and don't explain away an incident or sighting until we *know* the reason for it. If anyone has a suspicion or something they can't explain, *I* want to know about. Do I make myself clear? You all know the number to call."

There was a nodding of heads accompanied by "Absolutely, sir" and "Quite clear" as more notes were made.

He looked across at the Brigadier.

"Brigadier Johnson, I want your chaps who are detailed for security at Baltic, at Horton Lab and at this house to be on their toes. They are already doing a fine job, I know, but I want them all to be kept on high alert and to be briefed accordingly."

Johnson nodded his cooperation to the Controller.

"As you say, my men are already deployed but they will have a further briefing on their role in this exercise. I know we can have the utmost confidence on their response."

The Controller looked across to the DC.

"Deputy Commissioner, the same goes for the police. Your men on the ground are well placed for talking to the public and for moving around their patches and they may well get a sniff of something going on which is reportable. If that happens, I want to know about it."

"You can rest assured, Controller, that the Wiltshire Constabulary won't let us down. I've a meeting in

Trowbridge tomorrow when all my senior officers will be briefed on the situation."

The Controller turned in his chair to look down the table at Ali Jenkins who, up to this point, had been a fascinated spectator – albeit slightly concerned that she may have been invited to the wrong meeting.

"Miss Jenkins. I have intentionally reserved your input until now because I believe the contribution you'll be able to make will be most telling."

Chapter Seven

This abrupt introduction took Ali somewhat by surprise. After all, she felt, she didn't have any comments to make on a par with the professionals who had preceded her and her role was modest, amateur and untried. Then she became aware that the Controller was speaking.

"Would you please tell everyone who you are and what position you hold? I stress that everyone here is bound by the same Official Secrets Acts as you and everything you say will be treated in strictest confidence."

She wasn't used to being the centre of attention of such an august gathering and she felt rather flustered as the faces all turned to look at her.

However, she took a deep breath and began:

"As you've heard, my name is Alison Jenkins and I live at Barton Cannings. Seven months ago I was recruited into the GHQ Auxiliary, which is a secret, underground organisation whose aim is to provide armed resistance against an occupying enemy force in the event of an invasion. My unit, which is made up of seventeen civilian men and women from the surrounding villages, is one of many which form a network across southern England. As the leader of my unit, I plan and coordinate training exercises which make use of our local knowledge and we target places where we suspect the enemy will be most vulnerable."

DC Harding was clearly astonished at what he was hearing.

"Miss Jenkins, are you telling us that this initiative is being carried out independent of any other security operations? Shouldn't you be liaising with the police or the army?"

"No sir," Ali replied, "our instructions are to be totally self-contained. The presumption has to be that the police force and the army, as we know them, wouldn't exist if an invasion was successful. It would be our job to make as great a nuisance of ourselves as possible to the enemy."

Colonel Bridges could barely disguise his contempt. "Do tell us," he asked. "How does a group of amateurs intend to achieve this? I presume you've had *full* and *expert* training and guidance in the handling of firearms and explosives?" He posed the question, clearly anticipating from his tone that Ali had not.

"Oh, yes, Colonel. All of my unit have had unarmed combat and small arms training from the SOE and we have a small arsenal of rifles, Sten guns and a Bren gun which is secured in a disused underground reservoir. We can all strip down and reassemble our weapons and we regularly practice this in the dark. We also have a stock of plastic explosives as well as crude TNT, together with a range of different fuses and detonators."

Brigadier Johnson asked, "And what opportunities has your unit had to put this training into practice?"

"Well, Brigadier, I admit we'd like more time to try out the tricks that the SOE have taught us. However, we've managed to practice with our explosives and we've succeeded in demolishing several old telegraph poles and a chimney stack. So we already know that we can knock out communications and structures very effectively."

"I see. Do you have any idea of the type of targets you'd aim to hit to make the most impact?"

"Well, sir, we have already placed explosives beneath London Road and we've mined five bridges over the canal. These charges are all invisible to inspection but they can all be fired immediately it becomes necessary. I believe, if its impact you're looking for, Brigadier, the demolition of the principal routes that would be essential to an enemy advance northwards would make a very good start."

"Great scot!" exclaimed the Brigadier, "I had no idea your plans were so far advanced."

The Controller addressed the meeting.

"Thank you, Miss Jenkins, for that summary. Now, ladies and gentlemen, from what you've heard, you'll appreciate that Miss Jenkins' organisation is to be taken very seriously indeed – which is exactly what the Prime Minister had in mind when he instigated the formation of these units last year."

He looked across to Commander Pritchard and smiled.

"Commander Pritchard. I believe that, unbeknown to her, you've been aware of Miss Jenkins' activities and I understand that you've some information which all of us, particularly Miss Jenkins, will find interesting."

"Yes, Controller, I have. We've been watching her unit's training exercises for some time and we've been very impressed with what we've seen."

He turned to Ali. "Miss Jenkins, would you mind telling the meeting what your normal job is, please?"

Ali, who had been pleasantly surprised at Pritchard's compliments, was mildly startled at this sudden change of tack and she felt slightly threatened at having to disclose her humble occupation to such a high-powered group of professionals. Then she felt defiant. It was, after all, a very necessary job.

"I'm a part-time cleaner, sir."

"Thank you. Would you tell the meeting where you do your cleaning?"

"Yes, I work at Lynton House in Barton Cannings. It's a large mansion which is being used to accommodate a girls' private school that was evacuated there after they were bombed out of their place in London."

"And the name of the school – it's St Hilda's. Am I right?"

"Yes." Ali was becoming puzzled by the line of the Commander's questioning.

"Did you have to attend an interview with the headmistress to get this post?"

"Yes, although the head, Dr Madely, told me that I was the only applicant. She said she was relieved that I *was* suitable as she didn't know what she would have done to find someone else."

The Commander looked from the Controller to the rest of the group and then back to look at Ali.

"Well, Miss Jenkins, I have a small confession to make here. You see, we made sure you got this job because we arranged for you to be the only applicant by 'loosing' the letters from the four other applicants in the post!"

Ali gasped but, before she had the opportunity to make any comment, the Controller smoothly interrupted.

"Commander, would you please explain to us all why you wanted Miss Jenkins to be working at Lynton House?"

"Certainly, Controller. I want Miss Jenkins to keep a watchful eye on everything that goes on in that establishment. It just so happens that we suspect one of the teaching staff at St Hilda's school of being an enemy spy. I've already mentioned how clever some agents have been at hiding their true identity by being absorbed into the community and *this* person has been particularly skilled in infiltrating the school's set-up." He added, "Although that's not too difficult, when you consider that a private school is not subject to the same level of scrutiny as a state school."

From the mixture of expressions round the table, the meeting greeted this revelation with utter astonishment, including Ali, who nevertheless felt slightly annoyed that she had been manipulated in this way. However, she felt excited at the prospect of making an important contribution.

Commander Pritchard was about to continue with his explanation when DC Harding interrupted:

"Surely this could be putting people's lives at risk, including the pupils. Shouldn't you be telling Dr Madely about any of this?"

"Absolutely not, Commissioner! That's the *last* thing we want. This person we're watching is a very clever bird and I can't run the risk of Dr Madely suddenly changing her behaviour, however slightly, because she's in the know and, as a consequence, tipping off our friend that something was wrong. Rest assured, if this person had the slightest inkling that they were under suspicion, they could slip through our fingers or take action we might later regret."

"That's a high-risk strategy, Commander," said the Colonel, who had now become as engrossed as everyone else in Pritchard's proposals.

"You're right, Colonel, it *is* high risk – but it's a calculated risk. But when you weigh that against the intelligence that this person could be getting out of the country – and that includes details of the RDF development, the Baltic operation and the military build-up of an expeditionary force – it's a risk I believe we have to take."

"So, what happens now?" asked the Commissioner, with whom it was just beginning to register that he'd had no involvement in planning the arrangements which were unfolding in front of him. "Controller. Have you been privy to all of this?"

The Controller, still reclining in his chair, gave another relaxed wave of his hand.

"Commissioner, I have the utmost trust in Commander Pritchard's grasp of the situation and, yes, he has consulted me from the beginning on all aspects of this operation."

He then turned to the other members around the table. "Earlier this evening, I said that these were exceptional circumstances calling for exceptional measures and I believe you will now see that was no overstatement on my part. The very future of this country could be at stake! Prior to this evening, some of the information you've now all heard was shared by only a small number on a 'need to know' basis. But things have now come to a head, which is why each of you has been given the full story."

Then turning to Commander Pritchard, he apologised. "Sorry, Commander, we interrupted you. Pray, continue."

Pritchard was poised, ready, but had been waiting for the Controller's prompt.

"Thank you, Controller. So, we have a German agent who has succeeded in infiltrating the school as a member of staff. We have been watching this person from a distance for some time and our information is that things are likely to happen in the near future. What we wanted was to have a much closer contact with our friend and, when a teaching vacancy at St Hilda's arose recently, we managed to insert our own candidate – using the same tactic we used with Miss Jenkins' post – so we now have a permanent observer in place without, we hope, arousing anyone's suspicions of their real purpose."

"Can you tell us who the spy is or, come to that, who the watcher is?" asked the Commissioner. "Surely, we should know who they are?"

"Certainly not!" exclaimed Pritchard, who was clearly disappointed that the Commissioner hadn't grasped the need to prevent this from becoming known. "It's absolutely crucial that no one, other than our own agent on the staff, should know this person's identity!"

The Commissioner nodded. "Yes, of course. I see that now."

Turning to Ali, but addressing everyone, he added, "If Miss Jenkins knew who they were, there is just a chance she might unwittingly react in such a way as to put them on their guard. As it is, her ignorance of their identity will be her best defence."

He then added, "Having said that, Miss Jenkins, your best defence is to trust no one, however plausible they may seem to be."

"Yes," said Ali, "but what exactly do you expect me to *do*?"

"Miss Jenkins, we want you to watch and listen at Lynton House. We have selected you for this job because you are alert, resourceful and observant, as we've already seen. And you will now have gathered that you're also a 'member' of our intelligence family. And, while you won't be engaged in quite the role that you've been trained for, you're ideally placed to help with surveillance of the St Hilda's community. You'll be my second 'pair of eyes' at Lynton House. As the humble cleaner – and you'll forgive me for putting it that way – it's unlikely that anyone would give you a second glance. And yet, you'll have two important advantages over my observer, who is already there. You'll have unrestricted and unchallenged access to all parts of the building without giving rise to suspicion and, just as important, you are free to come and go from Lynton House, which will allow you the opportunity to report in to the Controller or to me, should the need arise."

"Will your man know that I'm working for you?" Ali asked.

"Yes, they will – although," he said, smiling, "who said anything about this person being a man? It could equally be a woman and, for the reasons I gave earlier, I'm not offering you any clues as to their identity."

"And how do I report in?"

The Controller resumed his role of directing the briefing and, in responding to Ali's question, addressed everyone round the table.

"Our aim is to capture this German agent and any information they may have intact. This operation will be codenamed 'Wansdyke'. You, Miss Jenkins, will observe closely the behaviour of *all* the residents at Lynton House and note anything which you feel is unusual or inexplicable. You will report this to me by telephone, using the existing dialling arrangement and asking for 'Auntie'. If you're told I'm unavailable, you'll report to Commander Pritchard on the same number by asking for 'Uncle'. One of us will always be here to take your call, day or night. I stress you must *not* use the telephone at Lynton House, as we suspect it's been intercepted. If all else fails, use your short wave transceiver."

"I understand, sir," said Ali.

"The rest of us will all have our parts to play in bringing this exercise to a successful conclusion."

Turning to the Brigadier and the Commissioner, he said, "The police and the army will need to be kept in a state of readiness, but without exciting undue attention. That's not easy, I know, but I'm confident I can rely on you both to make the necessary arrangements."

The Deputy Commissioner nodded. "That shouldn't be difficult for us. A select group of officers was seconded from divisions around the county only last week with the task of looking into new security procedures. Their function is already known within the force so they aren't going to attract more than the usual curiosity. I'll just add this operation to their remit and brief them on the need for top security."

"That sounds an excellent plan, Commissioner," said the Controller, who then turned to the Brigadier, inviting his input.

"Yes, Controller," he responded, "I can put up a platoon armed with a Bren gun carrier and a scout car in the area. I'll brief their lieutenant on the real purpose of their mission but, as far as the men are concerned, they'll be told they are taking part in manoeuvres as part of special training for a secret mission overseas. These chaps are extremely mobile and can react with the utmost speed."

"That's splendid," said the Controller. "It now remains for you, Captain Masters, to return to Baltic to resume your operations." He added, smiling, "By the way, the Deputy Commissioner assures me that you won't have any further visits from members of his force. You will, obviously, continue to exercise discretion regarding your activities – particularly regarding flights to and from the barn. And we all hope," he added, looking around the table, "that your hand mends quickly."

The Colonel agreed wholeheartedly, anxious to mend any rift he may have created earlier. "Absolutely, Captain Masters. And do be sure you get it seen to. Can't have our chaps walking around, wounded, y'know!"

Rosemary Masters smiled for the first time since the meeting had begun.

"Thank you, gentlemen, for your concern and good wishes. Controller, I've noted your advice, which I welcome and I shall contact you should I have anything to report."

This seemed to provide the signal for the meeting to finish and, with the scraping of chairs and the shuffling of papers, everyone stood, ready to leave.

Commander Pritchard took the opportunity to come round the table to talk to Ali and, as he approached, she noticed for the first time, what a tall, handsome figure he made. He reached out to shake hands.

"Miss Jenkins, I just wanted to congratulate you on your performance this evening." He gave her a quiet smile. "That couldn't have been easy for you, coming into such a highly charged meeting and I think everyone now gives you the greatest respect for what you've already achieved – and for what you will be doing."

Ali blushed with pleasure. "Not at all," she said, "although I have to admit it *was* daunting. I had no idea what to expect and I was very grateful for your help. So, thank you for that."

"No! It's *I* who must thank *you* for taking on this task. I can't overemphasise the importance of your role in all of this and the danger you may be exposed to. So, if you need any help or advice at any time, never hesitate to contact me."

So saying, he gave her hand another warm squeeze before wheeling away to retrieve his papers from the table.

In the meantime, the others were filing out of the hot and stuffy room into the cold of the large hall. Waiting at the door, the Controller was standing with an outstretched hand and he shook Ali's hand warmly.

"Miss Jenkins, that was absolutely splendid. I'd heard excellent reports from Commander Pritchard on you and your progress and I now see that his praise was entirely justified. I have every confidence that you'll do an excellent job for us!"

"Thank you, Controller, very much. I'll do my very best," she replied and went out to where her car was already waiting to take her back to Barton Cannings.

Chapter Eight

When the plane crashed, it shook the whole village – and in more senses than one.

On a night raid on Oxford, the Heinkel had been hit by flack before it could drop its lethal load and it had been trying to evade Spitfires which had been scrambled from their temporary base at RAF Abingdon to protect the city.

Disorientated and damaged, the German plane had been limping back on just one engine but, instead of heading due south for the coast, its injured pilot had mistakenly flown south-west and it was his misfortune to have encountered a lone Hurricane west of Swindon.

In the pale light of early Saturday morning the bomber flew at treetop level up the Kennet valley in a vain attempt to escape. It wove sluggishly on reduced power over the contours of the neighbouring downs before swooping down into the valley, east of Devizes.

In desperation, it opened fire on the Hurricane as it closed in, but the fighter's superior power and manoeuvrability made this futile.

With black smoke pouring from its remaining engine, the pride of the Luftwaffe sustained a prolonged burst from the Hurricane's cannon and its final act was to plunge vertically into a field, some hundred yards to the rear of a small row of houses in Barton Cannings.

It was initially engulfed in flames and smoke but, as its payload detonated, the flames were superseded by a series of blinding flashes as the aircraft disintegrated in a massive explosion, with debris covering much of the neighbourhood.

Farm worker, Jack Barker, had watched the closing stages of the drama from his bedroom window. He thought how lucky he'd been when he saw the plane just miss his house. He was killed instantly by the blast, which removed the roofs of two houses as neatly as if cut through by a cheese wire.

In the silence that followed the echoes of the explosion, the dawn air was broken only by the crackle of small flames which licked the edge of the blackened crater in the field and the occasional crack of exploding ammunition.

Of the pilot and his two gunners, there was no sign. Their bodies had fragmented with the rest of the plane and were spread over the neighbouring countryside.

For what seemed a long time, nothing happened.

Excepting a rare skirmish of fighters high above the village, residents had no first-hand experience of enemy action and it took some time to register with them that the massive explosion that had awoken them all had been close by and that it had something to do with the War. Even old Charlie Smith, who was stone deaf, knew something had happened

Such was the size of the explosion that it rattled windows in Devizes, four miles away, where ARP wardens on watch at the top of Wadworth's brewery could see, to the east, a plume of black smoke towering up into the morning sky.

Residents living closest to the crash arrived first, gradually to be joined by those coming from further afield. Some came running, some came on bikes and a few arrived by car – all wearing the nearest garments they could lay their hands on in their haste. One of them was wearing a torn mackintosh.

As each of them approached the scene they slowed abruptly as they took in with horror the devastation ahead of them.

Where previously there had been two, semi-detached farm cottages, there was now an ugly gap where one had been completely demolished. Excepting, that is, for one gable end, which defiantly remained upright. Beneath this, the space where the houses had been was now a pile of brick rubble, with large timbers poking out at crazy angles and, from some broken floorboards, pieces of patterned lino hung limply, like torn flags. A haze of dust and smoke hung in the air which contributed to a pungent smell which pervaded the atmosphere, getting into the eyes and throats of the onlookers.

After the initial pause, people started forward, frantic to look for survivors. From the edge of the gathering came an anguished wail and sobbing. Josephine Barker had just arrived and had suddenly realised she was looking at the remains of her parents' house.

"Oh, no!" she repeatedly sobbed, over and over as she was half supported, half-restrained by neighbours.

At this point, a perspiring PC Harper arrived. He stepped off his bike and reviewed the scene, taking in the smoking crater and the demolished house and the gable end.

"Oh, my God, what a bloody mess!" he gasped, and then realised he needed to take control of the situation before someone got hurt.

"Everybody, get back!" he ordered to those who had ventured to the edge of the wreckage. "Don't touch anything yet! That gable wall looks as if it could come down at any moment!"

Rick Scanton rushed up to him. "You silly bugger!" he shouted into Harper's face, "Jack and Mavis Barker are under that lot! We got to get them out!"

Emotions were running high and, from the same objection being raised by a few other voices, there was an obvious clamour for action.

"Right," said PC Harper, "this is what we do! For a start, Charlie, Jeff and you, Jessie," he addressed three bystanders, "watch that wall! Don't take your eyes off it and if you see it start to move, you yell bloody loud! D'you understand?" They each nodded vigorously and moved away to start their vigil.

Harper then turned to the group who had retreated from the rubble.

"Listen to me! We don't know how stable that rubble is. It's partly supported by those planks and they could collapse at any minute. Take out the loose stuff first and throw it well clear. Don't pull on any timber without warning the others." He then lowered his voice. "And keep listening in case there's someone in there who's still alive!"

He then went back to the rest of the gathering where people, who previously had been too shocked to show any emotion, were now openly embracing each other for comfort.

"The rest of you, keep well back. Edith." He turned to one of the women supporting a distraught Josephine Barker. "Take Josie home. Keep her warm and give her some hot sweet tea. Tell her husband what's happened and keep her there. We'll send you word if there's anything you need to know!"

At that point, Sergeant Bridewell screeched to a halt in a police car, accompanied by a constable from Devizes.

"Strewth! Just look at that!" was his first human, if not professional, reaction.

"Constable, what's happening?" he demanded.

"Sarge, a plane crashed into the field at the back of the houses and exploded. We believe that there are at least two people under that lot," he jerked his head towards the rubble. "There could be a third, but we're not sure. I've just organised a watch on that wall while they search the rubble."

"And what about the plane?"

"I haven't looked there yet, Sarge, but you can see the hole it made. I don't think anything could have survived that."

"You're right, Constable. Well done. Now, we'll have to keep these people back and clear the road for any traffic."

The sergeant looked around him at the growing number of villagers who were congregating on the road and grass verge outside of the garden hedge and who were watching in various stages of shock. Reverend Blunt pushed his way through the knots of people to where Sergeant Bridewell and Harper were standing and introduced himself to the sergeant.

"I'm Reverend Harvey Blunt, vicar of St Mary's. Is there anything I can do to help?"

Like the others, he'd dressed in the nearest clothing he could grab in his haste to get to the scene and he looked incongruously comical for a man of the cloth. Gardening trousers and a raincoat covered his pyjamas, topped and tailed by a tweed flat cap and wellingtons.

"Thank you, Vicar, but at the moment I don't think there is. I know it's very frustrating because we all feel we want to do something. However, I suspect you may be getting people who'll want to talk to you about this, so I suggest you could get ready to receive them at the church."

"That's a very sensible suggestion, Sergeant. I'll go and open up. If the opportunity arises, perhaps you'd let people know that's what I'm doing?"

Reverend Blunt threaded his way through the still growing crowd and left for the vicarage to change his clothes.

Sergeant Bridewell turned back to PC Harper. "Where's the nearest phone, Harper?"

"Just over the road at Hilliers, Sarge," he replied, pointing down the road towards the blacksmiths and the garage, run by the Hillier brothers.

"Right! I'm going to report in at Devizes. I'll see if I can get some more help – perhaps one of our contractors could spare a lorry to take this debris away. Has anyone called an ambulance?" His tone betrayed his feeling that an ambulance was unlikely to be necessary.

"Yes, I have," piped up someone. "That was fifteen minutes ago, so it should be here directly."

ARP Warden, Arthur Kemp, arrived in blue uniform and tin hat and Harper briefed him and directed him to supervise the search party on the rubble.

Bridewell turned to Harper. "We've got all the manpower we want and we don't want all these other people here now. Can you get them to leave? They know you and they'll listen to you."

As the sergeant began to walk towards the garage to make his phone call, PC Harper stood on the tallest mound he could find on the grass verge and called for attention. Gradually everyone stopped talking.

"Now, I know that what's happened here is a huge shock for us all and I know you all want to help. But we've got all the help we can safely use and the best thing you can all do is to go home and make sure you can account for everyone who lives with you. A lot of shrapnel and wreckage has showered onto our houses and property, so check that no one's been injured and that your property hasn't been damaged."

As an afterthought, Harper added, "And don't forget to have some breakfast and it's important that you get a hot drink. Things can look a lot better when you've had a cuppa."

The first ambulance to appear on the scene didn't come from Devizes hospital but from the American military hospital on Cannings Hill. The camp commander had heard and recognised the explosion for what it was and he'd immediately deployed medical help in the form of a large, six-wheeled monster bearing a red cross and a team of three medics. The vehicle came careering down the road with its siren howling, before it slowed to allow the retreating residents to get out of its path. It finally stopped beside PC Harper.

"Holy Moses! What hit *that* baby?" the black driver exclaimed as he saw the extent of the damage over the top of Harper's head. "Hi, bud," he added, looking down at Harper, "I'm Corporal Caleb Berkley of the US Army Medical Corps. My cap'n sent us out here 'cause he guessed you might just need some help." He opened the cab door and jumped down. At six feet eight inches tall, Caleb Berkley was a giant of a man who looked down on the constable.

Harper, who had never enthused about the local American presence, suddenly found his opinion changing with the comforting company of the ambulance and crew.

"Thanks very much, Corporal," he said, looking up at Berkley and shaking hands with the American. "I'm

PC Harper. What you see is the result of a German plane exploding in the field over there." He pointed to the smouldering crater.

"Believe it or not, that's the remains of a two-storey cottage. We know that two people are somewhere under that lot – possibly a third. Some villagers are helping to search the wreckage, as you see, but I'm worried that wall could fall in on them at any moment."

"Yeah, I can see that. But first, do you have anybody hurt at all? My guys are just great at field dressings."

"There are a few who have cuts and bruises from the initial explosion and they've moved back up the road. Some of them are bound to be in shock. P'raps you could check them over?"

Corporal Berkely briefed his medics, who grabbed medical kits and trotted back up the road to administer to the injured stragglers, and then he turned to look at the teetering wall.

"I guess we can help you with that, Mr Harper, if we could get some rope. I've got a cute little winch on the front of this baby," he said, patting the ambulance, "but I don't have enough cable to reach all that way."

Thirty minutes later, ropes had been rigged to Corporal Berkley's winch. The searchers were cleared from the danger area and, with just the smallest exertion from the winch, the wall came crashing down with a roar away from the collapsed house.

As this happened, a cream-coloured ambulance from Devizes hospital pulled in to the verge, dwarfed by the size of its American counterpart.

With the danger of the wall removed, work commenced with renewed energy to search the wreckage. After twenty minutes they found the mutilated remains of Jack Barker beneath some mangled roof trusses. The body was carefully placed on a stretcher and covered with a blanket before being lifted into the smaller ambulance, which drove off to Devizes.

Hot tea was distributed to the searchers, who then resumed their work, but with less optimism. It had now been nearly two hours since the crash and the initial adrenalin rush had subsided and the shock of the tragedy was hitting home.

Then there came a yell from the group on the far side.

"Quiet! Everyone shut up!"

Every one stopped moving. Then there was another shout.

"There's someone here! I think there's someone in here!"

There was a sudden frantic flurry of activity as the searchers renewed their efforts, shouting instructions, pulling at masonry, lifting planks and ripping away sheets of linoleum. Occasionally, there would be a pause to listen or to ease out a chunk of brickwork. Then they resumed their efforts. After twenty exhausting minutes, Mavis Barker was carefully extracted from the wreckage by the triumphant gang.

She was barely conscious. Her right arm and leg were broken and she had sustained a number of cuts and bruises.

Caleb Berkley took charge. "Don't you worry, lady, you're gonna be just fine!" he drawled as she was lifted gently onto the waiting stretcher. Turning to Harper, he said, "She's had a narrow escape, when you consider where she was found. We'll give her first aid here and run her in to Devizes hospital."

Having reported in by phone to Devizes police station, Sergeant Bridewell returned, just as the army ambulance turned round and drove away.

"Right, Harper. A team from RAF Upavon will get here eventually to recover whatever they can from the crash scene – although I can't see that they'll have much to take away. Our job is to check that everyone is accounted for. We need to check for any injuries to persons and damage to property and to coordinate the collection of any remaining debris from the plane. That could be a long-winded job because the blast will have spread stuff over a big area."

"OK, Sarge, I'll get started on that. I'll get our ARP warden to help with the house-to-house check and I'll speak with our headmaster to see how the schoolkids can help in collecting up the debris. They come from a wide area and they can use those sharp eyes of theirs to check round where they live. If there's anything to be found, you can be sure they'll spot it."

"That sounds good to me," said Sergeant Bridewell, who then paused, as though making a mental check of the police responses to all that had happened.

"I think we've covered everything at this end, so I'll leave you to tidy up. You'll get your report to me by

Monday morning, but be sure to contact me pronto if anything crops up that I should know about."

PC Harper found that, for the second time that morning, he was experiencing an unexpected affinity towards someone who he'd previously disliked. While Bridewell's words couldn't be construed as anything other than professional, they'd been delivered in a manner which made him feel he was part of a team.

With renewed energy, PC Harper set out for Barry Dyke's house.

Chapter Nine

On the Sunday following the plane crash, the residents of Barton Cannings were coming to terms with that event in every way possible.

A steady stream of friends and relatives of Jack and Mavis Barker had called on Jo to offer their sympathy and support. Some got car rides to Devizes to visit Mavis in hospital. Mavis, although greatly shocked and in considerable pain, was remarkably resilient and wanted to be discharged, although her doctors dismissed that totally.

The Reverend Blunt was not too highly regarded by many of his parishioners and, in normal circumstances, only a few people attended matins at St Mary's church. However, although he had expected a larger than normal congregation on this particular morning, he could not have anticipated the numbers who packed into every pew.

Pupils and some staff from St Hilda's school occupied the front rows and they were joined by many villagers – some in family groups, some with friends and some were on their own – but all wanting to join in an expression of united grief, not only for the death of one of their own but they also grieved and were angry for what had befallen their village.

They were even joined by a number of British and American soldiers and Ali was surprised to see Commander Pritchard sitting there, with some of his civilian staff.

The Reverend Blunt surpassed the expectations of everyone in his handling of the service. He was acutely aware that there were many strange faces in his flock that morning. Many hadn't been to church since last Christmas, some since last harvest festival – and there were some who'd never been to St Mary's, even though they'd lived in the village all their lives. But he recognised their need and he skilfully defused any discomfort and awkwardness they may have felt and he welcomed them all.

The service followed none of the formalities laid down for matins. Instead, it consisted of patriotic hymns interspersed with prayers for the Barker family, for villagers who were serving overseas and for those who awaited their safe return.

The sermon was a masterpiece – a mixture of comforting words of solace and stirring words of hope which left the congregation moved to face the future with optimism. Indeed, several of Blunt's biggest critics could scarcely believe that he had been capable of such an appropriate response. Before the final hymn, *Eternal Father, Strong to Save,* the vicar reminded his flock of the Spitfire fundraising party to be held at the school on the following Saturday, an event he was sure everyone would want to support.

Afterwards, it took some time for the large congregation to disperse, partly because it was difficult for such a large gathering to leave the church quickly but mainly because most people just wanted to use the opportunity to stop and talk. They lingered in groups of various sizes – some standing on the weed-strewn gravel path, others spilling out onto the grass between the gravestones. It was perhaps surprising that, even though the village had a small population, there were many residents who hadn't seen one another much during the dark winter months and here was a chance to catch up on how each was being affected by the War.

As Ali waited for her mother, who was in conversation with Rachel Stagg, she became aware of someone behind her and she turned to see the smiling face of Peter Pritchard, who quickly reached out to shake her hand.

He said in a low, urgent voice, "Act as though we are meeting for the first time."

Ali found she had responded automatically, and Peter Pritchard held onto her hand and drew her away from the nearest group of people so there was less chance of their words being overheard.

"Please listen carefully to what I have to say."

Ali glanced up at him before looking around her.

"There is every chance that the plane crash will have made our friend at Lynton House very jumpy. So keep your eyes peeled and let me know immediately if you notice anything unusual. There's just a chance he or she might use the distraction of this crash to do a runner with any information they've already got on the military build-up and on the RDF system – and that's the last thing we want!"

Ali played along with the pretence of the conversation and turned to Pritchard with a big smile.

"Yes, I can see how important that is. What do you want me to do?"

"Nothing specific. Just be aware that someone at Lynton House could do something which is out of character. I don't know what it'll be. It could be anything, but I'm sure you'll know it if you see it."

"Well, it's been very nice meeting you," said Ali, raising her voice for the benefit of anyone within earshot and reaching out to shake his hand. "I can see my mother's ready to go so I must give her my arm. She finds it difficult to walk very far on her own, you know."

He held on to her hand momentarily.

"Yes, it's been very nice meeting you, Miss Jenkins. We must meet again – over a meal, perhaps." His eyes twinkled and she suddenly realised she was looking at a very handsome man rather than at the head of counter-intelligence, and she became conscious of a stirring inside her that she hadn't felt since before Roy Boswell had received his call-up papers.

Slowly, the crowd broke up. First to leave was St. Hilda's school, with the pupils in an orderly crocodile, flanked by Dr Madely and Muriel Phelps.

Chris Edwards excused herself from the group and headed in the opposite direction to the telephone box by The Crown. She rummaged in her pocket for a piece of paper on which was written a Cheltenham telephone number. She dialled 0 for the exchange, gave the operator the number she wanted and waited. Eventually, she was instructed to insert her money and then she pushed button A to make her connection.

The coins crashed into the money box and she began her call.

"Hello, Bunty! It's me. Chris Edwards. Yes, it's lovely to hear your voice, too," she began and, after a few pleasantries in which she established that her friend, Bunty, was as well as could be expected and that she was coping with wartime education, she started to get some answers to a number of probing questions.

Chris listened intently to Bunty's responses.

"Bunty, are you absolutely sure about that? It's very important, you see, that there can be no mistake."

There was a pause as Bunty verified the details she'd just given to Chris Edwards who, in turn, had become quite tense with concern.

"Bunty, you've been a real pal as always, so many thanks for what you've told me. Oh! There go the pips! – I've got no more change so I'll have to ring off. – Do look after yourself and I'll call again soon. Bye."

She replaced the phone with a trembling hand and reflected on the information she'd just received before she left the kiosk and headed back to Lynton House.

Chapter Ten

Ali walked through the hall at Lynton House and down to the basement where she took off her overcoat and hung it in the cupboard before changing into her cleaning smock and her house shoes.

The room was warm and she could hear the boiler next door as it fizzled and hissed, like an oversized kettle, occasionally giving off a foul, sulphurous stench.

She picked up the large tin of Mansion polish and an assortment of rag cloths and a Ewbank carpet sweeper and then climbed the stairs to start her duties on the top floor.

Staff and pupils were usually all at breakfast at this time and Ali had found this was a good time to tackle the dormitories and staff bedrooms uninterrupted.

"Nothing's changed! Everything's normal," she kept telling herself, although so much had changed since her last day at work; first, the intelligence briefing, and then the plane crash.

As she reached the top of the stairs, she couldn't get out of her mind that anyone she saw at the school could be a Nazi spy.

There was a sudden loud bang behind her and Ali whirled round to see that the door to the airing cupboard had suddenly slammed shut. Hattie Perkins was standing there, balancing a large pile of ironed sheets on her arms.

"You all right, Miss Jenkins? You look like you seen a ghost!"

"Oh, Hattie," gasped Ali, holding onto the banister and trying to recover her composure. "I'm fine, thanks. It was just that door slamming behind me made me jump!"

"Lordy, I'm sorry! It does that sometimes. But I didn't mean to startle you. Mind you, it just goes to show. You've got to be so careful these days. You never know when someone's going to be creeping up on you," she laughed. "But at least we know that wouldn't happen *here*," she added, as she waddled towards the stairs, peering round the side of her precarious load.

Ali waited until she saw Hattie safely reach the first floor landing below before she headed along the carpeted corridor to Dawn Crosby's room to begin her cleaning.

This was her first day back and, although she'd been briefed to act as though nothing had happened, she was still coming to terms with the change in her role.

"Nothing's changed! Everything's normal," she repeated to herself again, giving the door a brief knock. As she anticipated, there was no reply and so she unlocked the door with her master key and went in, leaving the door open behind her, as was her normal practice. Hattie's warning had been given in all innocence, but it served to heighten Ali's state of awareness and she found herself occasionally glancing over her shoulder as she began to tidy and clean.

She saw nothing in the room to excite her interest. Miss Crosby appeared to be a tidy person. Her bed was made and her few clothes were either hanging in the wardrobe or folded neatly in the chest of drawers. A coat and a dressing gown were hanging on the back of the door.

On the small dressing table were two opened envelopes, both post-marked "Shrewsbury" and beside these was a small poster, advertising the Spitfire fund-raising party, which was due to take place on the following Saturday. Dawn Crosby's one suitcase was placed on top of the wardrobe.

Ali finished her dusting and she was in the process of checking that she was leaving the room as she'd found it when she heard a key being turned in a lock and, when she came out onto the landing, she was just in time to see Richard Kymer's door close.

This annoyed her a little because she'd intended to clean that room next, before anyone returned from breakfast. The only other rooms which could now be cleaned up there were Mr Gloyne's room and the room Chris Edwards referred to as her studio.

Ali felt this was always left in a mess, with paper and paints and part-finished models in papier maché and plaster of Paris covering every possible surface, including the floor. Indeed, it seemed that the success of all Art lessons was to be judged by the quantity of materials deposited on the floor and, since the budding artists were never encouraged to clean up after their forays into self-expression, it was left to Ali to scrape up the mess. She was annoyed because she knew she'd need the old scraping knife and the dustpan and brush for this job and they were still in the cleaning cupboard downstairs.

She closed and locked Dawn Crosby's door, pocketed her key and left the cleaning materials on the deep window sill opposite the laundry. She then went downstairs where she met Chris Edwards on the first floor landing.

"Good morning, Miss Edwards. If you're heading up to your studio, I haven't had a chance to clean it yet. But I'll be back up there to tackle it in a minute."

"Well, it's in a dreadful mess again, Miss Jenkins. But that *will* happen, of course, when the girls lose their inhibitions while expressing themselves. You are such an angel, even to *try* to keep it tidy for me!"

"That's what I'm here for," laughed Ali, and continued down the stairs to the basement, where she opened the cleaner's cupboard and collected her scraping knife and the dustpan and brush.

As Ali returned to the ground floor, a group of pupils came out of the dining hall, and passed Ali on their way to class, chattering and giggling as they went. Presumably, breakfast was finishing and she heard more voices in the hall, as pupils and teachers prepared to start the day.

One of the girls who'd just passed her stopped abruptly and thrust the books she was carrying into the arms of her companion.

"Hang on to these for me, please, Maureen. I've forgotten to get a book from Mr Kymer," she said, and went back into the hall.

Ali paused. "Maureen, you can tell your friend that Mr Kymer has just gone upstairs to his room. If she's quick, she'll be able to catch him before lessons start."

A puzzled look came over the girl's face.

"Thank you, Miss Jenkins, but Mr Kymer is still in the dining hall, finishing his breakfast."

For a fraction of a second, Ali thought she should correct her but, when she glanced in through the door, she saw Maureen's friend in conversation with Richard Kymer, who was still sitting at the staff table.

"How silly of me," she said with a laugh, "I must have been mistaken." She and Maureen exchanged smiles and Ali headed back up the stairs, her mind racing.

Ali knew that it was impossible for Richard Kymer to have left his room to get to the dining hall without passing her en route, and Ali knew that *that* hadn't happened. So who had gone into Kymer's room? Obviously somebody who had keys, but who could that be? And what other keys might this person have? And why should Kymer's room be of any special interest?

She then questioned whether she should go back and tell Kymer what she'd seen, but then immediately ruled that out. For one thing, she didn't want Kymer to know that she was anything other than a humble cleaner. If she could only have accounted for all of the staff in the dining room, she might then have been able to identify who was missing and deduce who this mystery person was. Chris

Edwards was the only person she *could* eliminate because they'd met on the landing while the person was still in the room.

Ali retraced her steps to the top landing and gave Richard Kymer's door an involuntary glance. It was still closed. She turned towards the art studio, where Chris Edwards was vainly attempting to rearrange her pupil's work into tidier bundles of clutter.

"It's lucky I've got this first period free so I can do a bit of preparation," she explained. "But I promise I won't get in your way." She began mixing some flour and water paste in a bucket and hummed tunelessly to herself as she went.

Ali ruefully surveyed the floor and began scraping the worst affected area. She'd made considerable progress when Chris Edwards, who had finished making her paste and had shredded large quantities of newsprint into a box, announced she needed to get something from her room below.

Ali swept the debris into a dustpan and dropped it into the waste paper bin. She looked back with some satisfaction at the clean floor and then moved on to the next area that needed her attention.

There were the sounds of learning all around. A teacher's raised voice, the scrape of chairs and pupils' chatter came up from the ground floor. From a more distant classroom came the rise and fall of collective laughter.

Then Chris Edwards came bustling back into the room, slightly breathless from climbing the stairs, her large bust heaving beneath the stack of boxes she was carrying. She stood, her feet planted astride as she recovered her breath, and she looked unusually agitated.

"D'you know, Miss Jenkins, I've just seen something rather strange. I was just reaching this landing when the door to Richard Kymer's room opened—"

Her words were abruptly drowned by a loud and unfamiliar sound. It came from outside the building – a continuous metallic squealing, accompanied by a raucous engine noise and it rapidly grew louder.

Chris Edwards' words momentarily forgotten, the two women moved quickly to the window to see what could be creating such a din. From their high vantage point of the top floor they could look down into the narrow road which wound past the school boundary. And, as they watched, a Bren gun carrier, carrying five men, come lurching into view, followed by an army scout car, equipped with a large machine gun.

As they grew closer, they saw that each vehicle had a tall, whip aerial which wafted around like drunken antennae. The young officer on board the carrier was wearing goggles and he had earphones clamped to his head and a microphone in his hand. A pair of binoculars hung on his chest.

As the carrier came to an abrupt halt, he stood up, but had to hang on to the vehicle to prevent himself from falling as it swayed violently on its rocking suspension.

At this point, Chris Edwards turned away and dropped her boxes onto a desk and, muttering something, quickly left the room. Ali remained at the window and saw the scout car screeched to a halt, narrowly avoiding a collision with the carrier. Through the open hatch of the vehicle poked the head and shoulders of another soldier, also equipped with earphones.

The commander of the Bren gun carrier had now produced a map which he examined closely before speaking into his microphone to give instructions to the occupants of the scout car. Then, turning to the front and speaking to his driver, he raised his arm and waved them forward.

With a renewed revving of engines, both vehicles lurched forward and passed from view. The road, Ali knew, ended at the farm just two hundred yards away so she knew they'd have to turn round to retrace their steps. And she was right. She had only to wait for a few minutes before the noisy vehicles came back up the road past the school and headed back the way they had come.

Ali felt excited by this intrusion into her day. It appeared that Brigadier Johnson had wasted no time in deploying his platoon to keep a presence in the area and she felt comforted at having them close by.

However, as the noise level in the building returned to normal, she recalled Chris Edwards' unusual behaviour. She had obviously been disturbed by something and had wanted to tell Ali about it, but the arrival of the army vehicles had prevented her.

Ali felt she'd done enough scraping for the time being and, leaving the art room, she prepared to tackle Eric Gloyne's room at the end of the landing. She knocked on the door and, when there was no response, she inserted her master key and entered.

She was greeted by a blast of cold air, which gusted through the room's open sash window, blowing sheets of paper into the air from the desk and causing the door to slam to behind her.

It was immediately clear from the room's appearance that Eric Gloyne was not a tidy person. The bed was unmade and clothes had been dumped onto the bed and left on the floor. To add to the impression of chaos, the whole room appeared to be strewn with sheets of paper – presumably due to the gale, which had been blowing through the open sash window onto the small desk beneath it.

Ali jumped forward and slid the window down and calm returned to the room.

It was impossible to clean without first trying to restore some sort of order and so, muttering under her breath, Ali began by sliding the papers to one side and making the bed and returning clothes to the wardrobe and the chest of drawers.

She then knelt down and picked up the papers on the floor and began stacking them into neat piles.

It was while she was concentrating on this task that she heard the floorboards creak on the landing outside and the door handle started to turn. She anticipated it was Eric Gloyne and she was preparing to explain to him why she was sorting his papers on the floor when she heard Christine Edwards call out, "He's still downstairs!"

Whoever held the door handle relinquished their grip and she heard the floor creak as the person retreated back along the landing. She scrambled to her feet, her heart racing, and rushed to the door but, by the time she'd wrenched it open, the mystery visitor was nowhere to be seen – neither was Christine Edwards.

Ali more was convinced that someone was snooping about this morning, although she could not be certain that it was the same person who had entered Kymer's room. Of course, it could have been one of the pupils who had called on Mr Gloyne, but this seemed very unlikely at this time of day. In any case, she thought, they would have knocked on the door first and then waited. They wouldn't have turned the handle without being invited to go in.

Preoccupied with these thoughts, Ali returned to finish off the job of restoring order to Mr Gloyne's room.

The last papers were scooped up to reveal a shabby carpet on a floor of loosely fitting boards, which proved a challenge to the squeaky Ewbank, despite Ali's best efforts.

As she cleaned the floor, she discovered a pair of socks which had escaped her notice under the bed and she bent to put them in the bottom drawer of the elderly dressing table. Yet when she pulled on the handles, the drawer refused to budge more than a couple of inches.

Ali gave the handles a firmer tug, but the drawer remained firmly wedged. So she bent down and ran her hand beneath the drawer to see if she could feel what was preventing the drawer from moving and her fingers touched something.

She knelt down to peer under the dressing table and discovered a large package had been taped to the underside of the drawer! Still in her kneeling position, Ali pulled on the drawer again and saw that the package was fouling the framework of the dressing table.

She immediately wondered what Eric Gloyne could possibly have that he wanted to conceal in this way.

At that moment, the bell sounded two floors below for the end of the lesson and Ali knew that Gloyne could be coming up to his room at any moment so she'd need to act quickly if she wanted to find out what the package contained.

With trembling fingers, she began to peel back the tape and it took precious moments before she'd eased away three sides of the package so that it swung down and hung, suspended by the fourth side and revealing its contents.

There were tightly folded papers covered in handwriting and diagrams. Stuck to these was a smaller document bound in brown card. Printed in black ink, it bore a spread eagle on a swastika and the words *Deutsches Reich* and *Reisepass*– a German passport! There was a miniature camera and the last item was a small glass bead containing a clear fluid.

From the general hubbub below, she could tell that classes were changing over for the second period and she thought she heard footsteps on the stairs. She had no time to investigate further and so, with her heart thudding, she secured it to its original position by pressing firmly on the adhesive strips around the edges.

Standing up, Ali grabbed her cleaning equipment and she was about to leave the room when the door opened abruptly to admit the large frame of Eric Gloyne.

"Ha! Miss Jenkins. Caught you red handed!" he said, then laughed and, although Gloyne was obviously joking, it made Ali give an involuntary jump and she felt her face go red.

Recovering quickly, she said, "Good morning, Mr Gloyne. Yes, I've just finished. I hope you don't mind but I've had to close your window. The wind was blowing those papers all over the place, so I've picked them up and put them back on your desk. I hope I've done the right thing."

"Miss Jenkins, thank you. That's really very good of you. I'm afraid I like a bit of fresh air in the morning but I forgot I'd left my window open when I went down to breakfast."

Ali was relieved to notice that at no time did he glance towards the dressing table. His sole concern appeared to be for his precious exam papers and he strode over to the desk to check the piles that Ali had made.

"Tip top! Miss Jenkins. That really is first class. Thanks very much for doing that."

He glanced over to Ali.

"I'd wanted a large drawer to keep those papers in and all they could give me was this dressing table. I didn't ask for it. And to cap it all, the damned drawer is stuck so it's no use to me at all! So I have to leave them on the desk."

He continued to gaze at Ali and she felt as if he was expecting her to reply. Was this a double bluff, Ali thought? But then he went back to the desk and put down his mark book and pen which seemed to signify the end of their conversation.

"Anyway," added Ali, smiling at Mr Gloyne. "At least they're all together again."

Ali left Gloyne's room, excited on the one hand by her discovery, and on the other hand wondering to what extent Gloyne's reaction was an act. If he *had* put the package under the dressing table drawer then he'd not reacted as she would have expected him when finding Ali in his room. She felt that she'd need to keep a further eye on Eric Gloyne.

Just an hour and a half had passed since she'd started work that morning and, already, there were a number of developments she felt she should report to Peter Pritchard. The thought of meeting the handsome commander again left her with a tingle of excitement as she turned along the landing towards Richard Kymer's room just as Kymer, himself, came out of his door with a number of books under his arm.

"Can I do your room now, Mr Kymer?" she asked, hoping her request sounded innocent enough.

Kymer gave her a beaming, trademark smile.

"Please help yourself, Miss Jenkins. I'm teaching for the next two periods so I won't be in your way."

Ali thanked him and went into his room, and she caught herself wondering why someone else had wanted to gain access so secretly.

The contrast with Eric Gloyne's room was remarkable, due mainly to its size and its state of tidiness. Being much smaller, the furniture gave it a more cramped feeling. But the bed had been made and there were no clothes in sight. However, being next to the large airing cupboard, the extra warmth made it rather stuffy and Ali felt that some fresh air would improve matters.

She went over to the window and reached over the desk to open the small sash window where she noticed a small groove had been cut into the window frame. She dismissed this discovery and set about dusting and polishing the furniture, checking under all the drawers as she went for any further concealments but, this time, found nothing.

The wardrobe contained a suit and a jacket on wire hangers and, on the shelf, was a trilby hat and a cap. On the top of the wardrobe was a large, battered suitcase and she noticed a smaller case which lay flat on the bottom of the wardrobe, partly covered by some shoes.

A raincoat and a dressing gown hung on the back of the door, covering a coil of wire, which she thought was strange. Ali checked the raincoat and was disappointed to find it was intact, without any tear. She then closely examined the contents of the chest of drawers, but these, too, appeared innocent enough.

Ali closed the window and retreated from the room, locking the door behind her.

On the first floor landing she met Hattie Perkins, who was puzzling over a list she was holding and scratching her head with a chewed pencil.

"What's up, Hattie?" she enquired lightheartedly. "Have they given you *another* problem to solve?"

"It seems that I'm now the domestic bursar as *well* as cook," she replied without looking up from her paperwork.

"Why, what's the matter? Is it something I can help you with?"

"That's kind of you, Miss Jenkins, but it's all to do with the furniture," she explained.

Ali immediately took a greater interest in Hattie's problem.

"You see," continued Hattie, "we had this extra furniture delivered last week. They said it was supposed to be second-hand but, if you ask me, it's olderer than that! And we got some new chairs. Some of our old ones were rotten as pears – full of woodworm, so I was able to move those down to the cellar. Anyway, Dr Madely asked me to do a re-shuffle of what we already had so as it spread fairer, like."

She looked up from her list. "All I've tried to do is to make sure each room had the same, so as no one could complain. The only thing was that every room is a different size and, when I brought in the new stuff, it didn't always suit 'cos they was either too big or too small for the room. So I changed some of the pieces round."

"Yes, Mr Gloyne said he had a dressing table that he hadn't asked for. So what's the problem?" Ali asked.

"Well, I gather that some folks have complained to Dr Madely. They didn't like the changes I done and they want their old furniture back as it were before. It makes me fair want to scream, I can tell you!"

"Oh, I shouldn't worry. If you kept a note of which pieces you moved from which rooms, surely it shouldn't be difficult to put them all back again. And I could give you a hand doing that."

Ali's mind was racing. If she could establish where Gloyne's dressing table had come from, she'd possibly know who'd taped the package under the drawer!

"If only it was that simple, Miss Jenkins. You see, I started to make a list. But now it's vanished. I'm sure it was here."

"Can you remember, for instance, where Mr Gloyne's dressing table came from?" Ali asked innocently.

"Sorry, Miss Jenkins, I can't. I've started to make this new list from memory, but it's hopeless. I can't remember who got what."

"Perhaps you could ask Dr Madely who had complained to her. You could then ask those people individually which piece they wanted returned."

"I thought of that but I daren't, Miss Jenkins. I'd look such a fool. Oh, dear, oh dear!"

"Well, if you need any help, you know you can count on me," said Ali, and leaving Hattie to puzzle over her list, she went downstairs.

She was about to head for the basement to change out of her cleaning overalls when Chris Edwards came out of the dining room. She appeared preoccupied and anxious.

Seeing Ali, she waited for two pupils to pass and then came over to her.

"Hello, Miss Edwards. Are you OK? This is the second time today that I've seen you looking worried. Whatever's the matter?"

Chris Edwards glanced furtively over her shoulder before replying. "Oh, Miss Jenkins," she whispered. "I don't know what to say. It's about this place. I'm certain there are things going on here. Things that shouldn't be happening. And I don't know who I can turn to."

"Gosh! Don't tell me that someone's having passionate affair with one of the teachers?" she laughed.

"No! Seriously! There's something I can't quite put my finger on. But I've seen things and heard things since I arrived here and they don't seem to add up."

"Are you sure your imagination isn't playing tricks on you?" Ali asked quietly. "I can't believe there's anything here that's out of the ordinary."

"That's just it," whispered Miss Edwards. "On the surface, everything looks normal. Everyone's so nice and polite and helpful."

"So what's caused you to think anything's any different?"

Before she could answer, Roger Jones sauntered out from the dining room, looking studiously at a book and nearly collided with them.

"Sorry, ladies!" he exclaimed. "My mistake. I should look where I'm going."

"That's all right, Mr Jones," said Ali brightly. "You were obviously stuck in that book of yours."

The two women laughed and stepped aside to let Roger Jones pass and only when he had disappeared round the corner of the corridor did Ali speak.

"Now then, Miss Edwards," Ali asked in a lowered voice, "what were you going to tell me?"

When Ali heard what Chris Edwards had to say, she headed straight out of the house to report to Peter Pritchard.

Chapter 11

When headmaster Barry Dyke arrived at eight thirty to unlock the school on the Monday following the plane crash, he carried a parcel under his arm wrapped in newspaper. He found that his infants teacher, dependable, punctual, middle-aged (and frumpy) Miss Phyllis Ponting was already waiting on the school steps.

"Good morning, Miss Ponting," he greeted her with less than his normal cheerfulness. He looked across the playground and past the dismantled fairground rides to where, two hundred yards away, was the pile of rubble which was all that remained of the Barkers' house. Men from RAF Upavon had already called to collect what remained of the crashed German plane and builders from Devizes were in the process of sorting through the rubble for materials which could be re-used. "What a dreadful thing to happen."

"I know, Mr Dyke," she gushed, "Absolutely dreadful. I feel so sorry for young Jo Barker, poor thing. As for all of our children, I'm worried about how they will be coping when they arrive this morning."

"Yes, that's something I'll need to discuss just as soon as Mr McIntyre gets here," referring to the second member of his staff. As if on cue, Wallace McIntyre turned into the school gate and cycled across the playground to join them.

"Good day, Mr Dyke," he greeted, taking off his cycle clips. "Hasn't this been an awful weekend?"

"It has indeed," Dyke replied, "and I need to talk with you both just as soon as you've hung up your coats. We need to be ready for when the pupils start to arrive."

Dyke knew he was fortunate to have two such dependable colleagues. Phyllis Ponting was the longest serving and he'd inherited her when he arrived at the school. This had been her first and only teaching appointment and it appeared that, during her twenty-three years at Barton Cannings, she'd taught most of the parents in the village as well as their off-spring.

Wallace McIntyre, on the other hand, was a relative newcomer, and had arrived soon after Dyke's appointment.

Despite their close association as teaching colleagues in the confines of such a small school, they were never on first-name terms, which was a source of amusement to some of the village.

"There are a number of circumstances we have to prepare for." Dyke addressed McIntyre and Miss Ponting a few minutes later in the seniors' class room.

"Firstly, parents will probably be looking to us to take a lead on how to respond to this dreadful disaster. The younger children and the infants are likely to be least affected, but we should anticipate that those in the top two classes will be suffering from some sort of delayed shock."

"How should we deal with this, Mr Dyke?" asked Miss Ponting, who'd had no previous experience of dealing with the affects of trauma on this scale.

"To start with, I believe we must carry on as normally as possible and under no circumstances should we convey any concerns or worries we may have to the children. It's likely that most of them will be able to cope if we keep to our normal timetables and keep their minds occupied, although there may be one or two who might be upset at what happened and might want to talk about it. In these cases, we can only play it by ear. But it will be important that we do listen to them and give them reassurance that they are safe."

"What about the school building?" asked McIntyre. "We must have been in a direct line with the blast. It's strange that Mrs Scarrott's caravan was closer to the crash and yet it escaped any damage."

"Yes, we were very lucky. Fortunately, there was no structural damage and Mr Mortimer came in on Saturday and did a splendid job in patching up the windows. You'll see that some are still broken, and he'll mend these just as soon as he can get some replacement glass." Miss Ponting and McIntyre looked round at the cardboard blocking a few broken panes in the windows and nodded their approval at the achievements of the caretaker.

"It must have taken him some time to clear up the mess," said McIntyre.

"It did, and it wasn't just pieces of glass. There were bits of the plane, bricks and roofing slates from the Barker's house – and some other bits I'd rather not talk about." His face grimaced with an expression of distaste and, once the others realised what he was referring to, they followed suit.

"And that brings me to my next point. Constable Harper has already been to me to ask if the children can help with finding any plane parts in our neighbourhood. Goodness knows, there must be fragments spread all over the village."

Wallace McIntyre frowned. "Surely, he's not asking us to let the children to go out searching during school time, is he?"

"No. This would have to be after school. But it would have to be organised properly. I shall explain to the children that, if they want to help, they will first need to have their parents' permission and they would need to stay in groups at all times – say, of four or more."

Miss. Ponting nodded her approval. "Yes, that would be just how we've been organising the waste paper collections, so I'm sure that their mums and dads would find that acceptable."

"What should they do with the bits that they find?" asked McIntyre. "I don't suppose the police want these to disappear into the private collections of small boys."

"There is always that possibility, of course," smiled Dyke. "No. I'll make sure each group includes a responsible senior pupil who will need to keep a strict eye on anything they find. This will then have to be taken to the police station and Constable Harper will take it from there."

"If they find any body parts, I suppose they'll need to be told to leave these and tell the police where they are?" asked McIntyre. Miss Ponting pulled a face of distaste at the mention of human remains.

"Yes, quite so," said Dyke. "Now, we shall have the pleasure of Constable Harper's company anyway, this morning, as he wants to talk to the children about the dangers of unexploded butterfly bombs."

"I saw a leaflet on the post office noticeboard about these," interrupted McIntyre. "Yet another evil little contraption produced by Hitler's boffins. They are dropped in clusters, y'know, and it seems they hang under a sort of canopy as they fall."

"Gosh," exclaimed Miss Ponting. "What dreadful thing will they think of next?"

"Yes," continued Dyke, "these are anti-personnel bombs. It appears that they are extremely unstable and just the slightest disturbance will set them off. Sadly, a number have been found by youngsters who have been killed by them as a result of their curiosity – and we don't want that happening to any of our children here."

"Certainly not," said Miss Ponting and Wallace McIntyre nodded enthusiastically. "Of course."

Outside, voices in the playground signalled the arrival of the first pupils, the younger ones accompanied by concerned mothers, who were giving their children words of encouragement.

"The next thing I wanted to mention is the Spitfire fund-raising party, which is arranged for next Saturday. Now, some may think it's rather distasteful to go ahead with this after what's happened here but, I for one, feel even more strongly that it should take place."

"I couldn't agree more, Mr Dyke," said McIntyre. "We can't let this crash, however tragic for the Barker family, prevent us from supporting the War effort. It certainly wouldn't be good for moral if we cancelled. We know the vicar's extremely keen to go ahead and I think that will be the view of most people in the village."

"Yes, it'll be a good opportunity for the community to come together and have some enjoyment, for a change," added Miss Ponting. "Our band has been practicing and we're looking forward to it."

The band that Miss Ponting referred to comprised the most unlikely combination of talent. Miss Ponting, herself, played the drums – nothing showy, just a very strict tempo for waltzes and quicksteps. The two Jessop sisters were accomplished violinists and Freddie Eden gave added substance with his flamboyant piano accordion playing – although he could only play tunes in the keys of C and G. The result was, nevertheless, very pleasing and, in the absence of any other form of musical entertainment in the village, the band was in demand for any concerts or dances held at the school.

Miss Ponting had been eyeing the parcel lying on Dyke's desk.

"What's in that?" she asked bluntly.

Dyke leant across and found the end of the newspaper wrapping. He gave it a yank like a conjuror and, with a loud thud, onto the table rolled a blackened block.

The two staff looked surprised and baffled. At first glance, it resembled a large brick but its surface was covered with charred flakes.

"That," declared Dyke, "is a German loaf!"

"But it's burnt and rock hard," remarked McIntyre, who'd picked it up and was examining it closely. He hefted it in his hand. "And it feels very heavy." He sniffed it. "And it smells strange, too."

"You're right on all counts – and it's apparently what the people in Berlin are queuing in their hundreds to buy, that is if they've got the money to buy it. I'm not sure what went into its making, but I'm told the ingredients contain very little in the way of wheat flour and it provides very little sustenance. "

"Strewth," McIntyre exclaimed, "I wouldn't want to have to eat it."

"Precisely so, and I think everyone who sees it will feel the same, which is why I've been asked to show it to the children." Dyke paused. "I'm not one to get involved in the propaganda business, as you know, but it's been suggested that, if the children could see that," indicating the object, "they may not think so badly about the food rations they're getting here."

Dyke glanced up at the school clock. "OK, let's get everybody in and we can start the day with assembly, as usual."

The day progressed surprisingly smoothly. PC Harper arrived and gave his warning about the danger of the butterfly bombs. Barry Dyke showed the children the loaf and explained why they were so lucky to have the food rations they were getting. Three teams of willing searchers were organised. Then, after assembly, everyone filed away to their classrooms where they were immediately and wholly engaged with their lessons.

Dyke's strategy of keeping to the normal routine seemed to work well and, except for Muriel Smith, who had one of her tantrums in which she succeeded in knocking over the class ink dispenser with unfortunate consequences, there were no incidents directly relating to the crash.

At the end of school, those in the search parties waited in their groups in the playground for their instructions from Wallace McIntyre. The infants were met by relieved mothers while the remainder went home in their usual twos and threes – all, that is, except Alfie Barter, who left alone.

Alfie wanted to do some searching, but he'd no intention of being stuck with a group. So he headed off on his own towards some fields near the scene of the crash on Bourton Lane, which were bounded by tall elm trees.

He started his search by wandering about in the open field and, after a few minutes, he came across a small, twisted fragment of bright metal. He examined it minutely, turning it over and over in his ink-stained fingers before putting it carefully inside his empty gas mask box.

Excited by his find, he continued his search, realising that it would soon be dusk and difficult to see clearly. He then found a small length of polished steel rod attached to a short cylinder. It looked very important and he cleaned this off against his trousers and stowed it with his earlier find.

Although he scanned the ground around him for some time he found nothing else until, in the fading light of the early spring evening, he kicked something in the grass with his foot. He bent down and picked up a round dial attached to a short length of copper piping. He'd seen something similar on his brother's tractor and he was excited because he knew it was a gauge of some kind, although he couldn't make out the printing on the dial's face.

The dial he crammed in with his other finds inside his box, which now hung down heavily under their combined weight. He felt very satisfied with the results of his search but knew he'd better be getting home if he was to avoid another ticking off from his mother and so he headed towards the field gate. Just as he was climbing over it he saw, stuck in the hedge beside the gatepost, the back of a brown flying helmet, complete with goggles. This, he reckoned, would be a real trophy to boast about and so he climbed down again and reached in through the thorns and brambles to retrieve it. It was rather heavy and he had great difficulty in pulling it free. He lifted it up to examine it closer, only to recoil with horror, dropping it hastily to the ground. For the helmet still contained the severed head of its former owner.

He leant against the gate for support, breathing deeply and feeling slightly sick and dizzy.

It took several minutes for him to recover sufficiently to think about what he should do. Then he remembered Mr McIntyre's instructions to the search parties and while, on another occasion, he might have ignored these just to be different, he realised that he'd have to report what he'd found, including the trophies inside his bulging box.

He re-climbed the gate and when he jumped down on the other side he nearly collided with a man who was standing in the gateway.

"Crikey, mister, you gave I a fright!" he exclaimed, still panting from his initial shock. "I didn't see you standing there."

"Sorry, young man," he replied. "I didn't mean to startle you. I hope you haven't hurt yourself?"

The man's voice seemed cultured to Alfie, with no trace of an accent, and Alfie knew he was not from around Barton Cannings.

Alfie brushed down his trousers and jumper. "No, I'm all right. Now I've got to get home or else I'll be in trouble with my mum. "

"I'm on my way back into the village, too. I'll keep you company, if you like." So saying, he turned towards the village.

"Would your name be Alfie, by any chance?"

Alfie swung round, surprised that this person should know his name.

"We've been told not talk to strangers," he said defiantly. "What's it to you, anyway?"

Alfie started off down the lane towards the crossroads but the man fell in beside him and Alfie was beginning to feel uneasy with this man's close company.

"Oh, I'd just heard that you were a clever lad. You obviously knew where to look for bits from the plane, for instance. None of the others came to look here, did they?"

Alfie felt more relaxed at this compliment. "No. Mind you, there aren't many places in the village that I don't know better than they."

"You must see lots of things that the others don't see."

Alfie's confidence began to flood back. Here was someone who was interested in him, Alfie Barter.

"Yes, I could tell you a few things about what goes on around here."

"Really?"

"Yes. For a start, take old Ma Scarrott. D'you know? She keeps stuff in a tin under her bed. I've watched through her caravan window and I seen her getting it out."

The stranger thrust his hands deeper into his raincoat pockets. "Does she really? That's clever of you to have found that out," he said encouragingly. "What else can you tell me about?"

"Well, there *was* something I seen only the other night. I were takin' a pasty up to our dad..."

At that point, the large figure of PC Harper loomed out of the dusk.

"Is that you, Alfie Barter? Your mother's waiting for you at home with your tea. So you'd better get back there, sharpish. Off you go, now!"

Alfie's companion, meanwhile, wheeled round and began walking away and, as he did so Alfie saw a large tear in the back of his raincoat. Within moments, the man was swallowed up in the gloom and Alfie was left standing with PC Harper.

Alfie grabbed the constable's arm. "That's him! That's him!" he whispered hoarsely, shaking Harper's arm in a state of excitement and pointing in the direction taken by the stranger.

"Alfie! Calm yourself and let go my sleeve," he said, prising Alfie's hand away.

"But, that's him, Mr Harper. That's him. That's the man with the torn coat what I seen up at Baltic!"

"Calm down, Alfie. Calm down. Now are you telling me that the man who's just been talking to you is the same man that ran from the barns at Baltic and tore his coat on the wire?"

"Of course it's him – and we're letting him get away." His voice was now an anxious whine.

"How can you be sure, Alfie? You told me before that you didn't get a good look at him."

"Well, it's the same colour raincoat, and it's got the same kind of straps with buckles on his sleeves. *And* the hat was the same."

"Right, young'n. You get off home straight away. I'm going to make a phone call then I'm coming up to your house to have another chat."

150

Alfie protested. "But I haven't told you about this stuff I found," pointing to his bulging gas mask box, "*nor* about the head in the helmet. That was real nasty!"

At this revelation, the constable hesitated.

"A head, you say?"

"Yes. It's in a flying helmet. I left it by the gate."

"Well that's going to have to wait if I'm going to apprehend this stranger. You go straight home and wait for me there. And don't stop to talk to anyone. D'you understand?"

With that, PC Harper mounted his bike and set off for the police station and a telephone while Alfie turned and headed home.

Harper's journey was uneventful and he saw no one en route. Breathing heavily, he left his bike in the road and dashed into his small office and grabbed the phone and called Sergeant Bridewell at Devizes.

This was going to be a very interesting evening.

Meanwhile, at Lynton House, while staff and pupils were engaged with supper, a phone call was being made to a London number. When it was eventually answered, the caller cupped their hand round the mouthpiece and whispered, "It's me. I need to know if we've got anything on a woman calling herself Christine Edwards or on another called Alison Jenkins."

Chapter 12

As Constable Harper was reporting to his sergeant, another call was being made from the village. Ali Jenkins used her special code, asked for "Uncle" and was quickly connected to Commander Pritchard at MI6.

"It's good to hear your voice." No name – just the acknowledgement – but the pleasant tone of his greeting sounded genuine, which made Ali more excited than she'd anticipated or wanted to admit.

"I've a number of things I need to report," she blurted.

"Then we need to meet up to talk. I can pick you up from Cannings crossroads in twenty minutes. You can make that?" Once again, it was more of an instruction than an invitation.

"Yes. That'll be fine."

"See you in twenty minutes, then." The line went dead.

Ali cycled home to tell her mother another white lie and then headed back towards the crossroads. She passed beneath the avenue of overhanging lime trees as she approached the junction where, for safety, she left her bike in the laurel bushes at the entrance to the vicarage. As she waited in the dark she heard another convoy of army lorries as it ground its way along London Road above the village. Overhead came the rhythmic throb of heavy bombers heading south on another sortie.

It was not until a further forty minutes that Pritchard arrived at the wheel of a small Ford car. He drew into the side of the road and leant across to open the passenger door for her.

"Hop in," he said, smiling, and Ali slid into the passenger seat beside him. When she closed the door, she found that the front seats were close together and she felt a tremble of excitement as her shoulder made contact with Pritchard's side as he reached for the brake

"Sorry to keep you waiting," he said over the noise of the engine, "but I was delayed by a phone call from the police. I'll tell you about it in a minute but, first, I need to find somewhere quiet where we can talk without the racket of this engine."

He turned the vehicle and headed up the road towards West End and, after just a few minutes, found a turning off the road onto a cart track. He reversed the car up the track until it was beneath the cover of some overhanging trees. He dowsed the lights, stopped the engine and turned in his seat to look at Ali.

There was a momentary silence as they both registered their closeness in the privacy of the car.

"Can we dispense with formalities when we chat like this?" he asked quietly. "If you're OK with that, please call me Peter and can I call you Alison?"

Ali hesitated and stared straight ahead. She'd not sat so close to an attractive man for a long time and she was hoping that she was managing to conceal the stirring she was now feeling inside her. He was so bloody attractive and she realised she wanted him.

"Yes, that's fine with me, although I'd prefer you called me Ali," she said quietly, turning to look at him. In the dark interior of the car she could just make out his face and his encouraging smile.

"Well, that's an excellent start," he said, briskly. "Now then, tell me about what's been happening at Lynton House."

Ali recounted the events of the day and Peter Pritchard listened intently, occasionally nodding as the details were set out for him.

"So, if I can summarise what you've told me. Our friend has stowed a package under a drawer of a dressing table which has then been re-allocated to another room. The package would appear to contain documents – almost certainly details of the RDF developments at Horton Lab – a German passport and a miniature camera. The glass bead you described was almost certainly a suicide pill. It would appear that the person responsible for putting it there is now searching the rooms to find this furniture and so reclaim the package." He paused for Ali's nod before continuing, counting off the remaining points on his fingers.

"You believe that Chris Edwards can be ruled out of having any involvement, but that she has witnessed an event which might be significant to us. You don't believe Gloyne is involved, but you can't be certain. Using Perkin's list, it may be possible to trace from where Gloyne's furniture was moved, and so identify who our spy is. And Kymer has an unexplained coil of wire in his room and so could be involved, but we don't know how. Have I missed anything out?"

"No, I think that covers everything." She hesitated. "Oh, yes. I should have mentioned that Brigadier Johnson's men have started their patrols in the village. A platoon came down the lane past the school today and so they now know where we are, if needed."

"That's very reassuring. I didn't think he'd waste any time in setting that up. As for your report, Ali, you've gathered some valuable information and what we've got to do is make best use of it."

Ali was grateful for the compliment. "What about the package? I presume I did the right thing in leaving it in Gloyne's room?" she asked, looking at Pritchard. "I thought that if I took it, it would tip off our friend that we were onto him... or her." Then she added, "As it is, we know the spy will want to get it back and so all we have to do is keep watch and then nab them in the act."

"You're absolutely right to leave it, Ali. For one thing, we know that the agent can't leave the country without it, so he or she must still be with us. But I think it will be more useful if we just keep watch to identify who we're dealing with. You see, once we know who it is, it'll be reasonably easy for my team to keep tabs on them."

Ali turned a little in her seat to face Pritchard, then looked down at her lap. "Yes, I see that now. How silly of me not to think that through." Then, looking back at him she asked, "Now, what were you saying about a phone call from the police?"

He was about to answer when he caught sight of a movement in the driving mirror and became aware of the silhouette of a figure striding towards them down the track from the field.

"Damn. There's someone coming! Ali? Quick. Kiss me!" he said and, grabbing her around her shoulders, he pulled her to him.

Momentarily startled, Ali turned her face up to his and then found herself kissing him, first with uncertainty and then with genuine passion. He responded fiercely, his tongue probing inside her mouth and he pulled her even closer to him, his hand exploring the contours of her body.

Her heart was pounding and her whole body was alive and she was now responding to his embraces. Their mouths met again as she pulled his head down towards her and his hand slid inside her coat to her breasts.

The sound of swishing footsteps in long, wet grass grew louder as the person came up to the side of the car and paused, before continuing on their way into the gloaming.

It was some time after the nocturnal walker had gone that they stopped. The windows had steamed up with condensation and they were both breathless and trembling. Ali was reluctant to let go and it seemed that Peter Pritchard, also, had more than intelligence gathering on his mind.

"Wow, Peter. Did they teach you that at MI6 training?"

"I was just going to ask you the same about the SOE!" he laughed. "But I didn't want anyone to recognise us and I couldn't think of any other way of hiding our identities."

Ali pushed him away to arm's length. "Are you telling me that you only did that for King and country?" she chided him.

Pritchard chuckled. "Well, I suppose it was but, in any case, I've been wanting to do that ever since I saw you at the briefing. I just didn't expect that it would happen like this."

He leant over towards her and pulled her closer. "But *this* is not part of any training manual," he whispered, and pulled her mouth to his as their hands became busy in exploring each other.

It was the intrusion of the hand brake and the gear leaver which finally intervened in their exertions and, gasping for breath, they sat back in their seats and gazed at each other.

Pritchard's heart was thumping. Since his wife had died in a bombing raid on Liverpool he'd found solace by immersing himself in his work, almost to the extent of becoming a recluse. His dealings with women had been restricted to working with those on his staff and he'd certainly not allowed himself to be distracted by any romantic dallying.

Now, in the confines of the small car, his suppressed urges had been suddenly re-awakened by the physical contact with this very attractive woman and he was surprised at his rapid erection in response to her clever probing.

"Well, I certainly didn't see that coming," gasped Ali, pulling down her dress. "I'd been expecting quite a different kind of briefing!"

"Me, too," Pritchard panted, "but I hope you don't think I took advantage of you in any way, although I can't say I'm sorry that it's happened. It's been a long time since I've been made to feel like I do now."

He paused and Ali sensed he was reflecting on some previous loss. She reached over to touch his arm.

"Peter, you've nothing to apologise for. It seems we're both in an emotional pickle and I'm glad we've found each other because I've been wanting you for some time, too."

She was surprised at her own frankness and no longer felt embarrassed about revealing her feelings.

"Isn't it strange how things have turned out?" reflected Pritchard, with a smile. "One minute I'm chasing Nazi spies and, in the next, I've caught a gorgeous woman."

"Well, I hope I'm not too big a disappointment for you," chided Ali. "After all, I'm sure a spy would have been a far better catch!"

"Yes, you're probably right," he laughed and Ali punched his arm hard in retaliation.

He winced and she laughed. "That serves you right for being mean. Now, what were you going to tell me about a phone call from the police?"

Pritchard groaned at being brought back to the present.

"Christ, you're right. For a moment I'd completely forgotten about that. Just see the effect you've had on me."

He then outlined the conversation he'd had earlier in the evening.

"I had a call from an Inspector Mansell at Devizes police HQ. His sergeant by the name of Bridewell had received a report from a PC Harper here in Barton Cannings. Apparently, the same boy who witnessed the plane at Baltic has been involved in another incident. It seems that he was returning from scavenging for plane parts this evening when he was approached by a stranger who started to quiz him on his activities. Alfie – that's the boy's name – became uneasy about this man's interest in him and he was ready to make a break for it when the two of them bumped into our patrolling bobby."

"Who was this man?" Ali asked. "Did Harper question him?"

"Unfortunately, no. To be fair to Harper, he was far more concerned with Alfie's story about finding a severed head in a flying helmet. So I can understand why he'd be distracted and didn't prevent this man from slipping through his fingers."

"Yuck! How gruesome! That sounds just like Alfie Barter you're talking about. Still, it's a shame PC Harper didn't nab our mystery man. What do you think he was up to?"

Pritchard paused. "He was pumping Alfie for information, for a start. That concerns me a lot because this person may have somehow found out that Alfie saw him at the Baltic barns and, if that's the case, he may suspect that Alfie can identify him. So Alfie's life could now be in danger."

"D'you think he was our spy – or could it be that there's somebody else involved?"

"That's a good question and, to be honest, I'm not sure I know the answer. The problem is that neither Harper nor Alfie could describe him in detail. It was only by seeing the torn mac that Alfie realised he'd been standing next to the man he'd seen at Baltic. So this bloke can disappear and be absorbed back into the community and we're none the wiser. What an absolute bugger!"

"But surely he'll stand out as a stranger," said Ali.

"In normal times that would be true," said Pritchard, "but these are hardly normal times. There are so many new faces in the area with contractors, engineers, civil servants and all the other people doing work for the government. So there's plenty of scope for him to go unnoticed as just another civilian working for some arm of the War Department."

"But you forget. He could even be a teacher at Lynton House. After all, no one other than Alfie and PC Harper have seen this person."

"Yes, there is that possibility and it's an obvious starting point." Pritchard paused for a moment.

"Ali, I want you to go back to Lynton House and carry on with your search. You say you've several more staff bedrooms to check out and, who knows, that may turn up something."

Ali nodded. "Yes, I'll do that. But that doesn't give me much time."

Peter Pritchard tensed in his seat. "Oh? Why's that?"

"Well, Dr Madely has decided to give the pupils an extra holiday. They've already had their half-term holiday but she feels that they need an extra break to get over the recent events."

"But how can that affect us?"

"Well, most of the children will be away from next Friday. Only a few seniors are staying on for the Spitfire party on Saturday. So, from Friday until the girls' return on Tuesday, the only people in the building will be teaching staff and domestics. And the teachers will almost certainly spend most of their time in their rooms, which doesn't give me much opportunity to do any searching without being seen."

Peter Pritchard looked concerned. "Yes, you're right of course. The last thing we want is for you to be seen creeping about the building. That'd certainly give the game away! You'll just have to get your searches finished before Friday while you're cleaning. That gives you three days. D'you think you can do it?"

"I'll just have to, won't I?" she replied, "and I'll keep you posted on what I find. If only I could trace Hattie's furniture list. That could hold the key to the business about Gloyne's dressing table."

"Yes, but whatever you do, take great care. We can only assume that no one has rumbled you."

"Oh, I intend to," she said, smiling and sliding her hand up the inside of his leg, "because I'm already looking forward to my next briefing and I want that to be far more extensive!"

He gasped at his sudden arousal and pulled Ali to him again.

"I can promise that I'll make certain of that," he laughed. "Now, I'd better return you to the crossroads before they send out a search party! I'd hate them to find you in compromised circumstances. Whatever would the village think? And, of course, mum's the word about Alfie's meeting with this man."

Meanwhile, back at Lynton House, a length of wire was being lowered from an upstairs window.

Chapter Thirteen

The cold, easterly winds which had prevailed for the first two weeks of April had, at last, abated, giving way to the warmth of spring. Blackthorn bushes were covered in white blossom, cowslips and primroses bloomed in abundance, hedges were suddenly green and chestnut spikes were rapidly forming. These were the signs that had, for generations, told country folk that the winter was behind them and these same signs gave the villagers at Barton Cannings a feeling of normality.

Lambing had finished. The fields of spring wheat on Chambers' farm were being rolled by one of the Land Army girls. Even the muddy tracks from the fields used by the milking herds had now dried out, making life easier for the elderly herdsman and his two Land Army assistants.

On the garden allotments, where the ground was, at last, workable, George Barter had joined other villagers who were busy digging in rotted dung, dibbing in their potatoes and planting their valuable vegetable seeds. The posters exhorting the nation to "Dig for Victory" were being taken very seriously in the village.

Spring was also having an effect on some of the younger men and women. Rick Scanton had noticed the tight blouse being worn provocatively by Daisy Hale but he'd received a sharp reprimand from her mother for his obvious attentions, while other village youths were ogling, with renewed interest, the girls in their spring dresses.

Yet, despite the diversion of these seasonal activities, the War remained ever present. There was the constant, throbbing drone of aircraft formations overhead – many were towing gliders – and the relentless roar made by an increasing number of tanks, half-tracks and army lorries on the roads around the village.

Villagers watched bemused as more and more British and American troops, in full battledress and straining under the weight of heavy packs and webbing pouches, clomped through the village on fitness runs, urged on by barking NCOs.

Regardless of the season, it seemed, the War went on – but everyone sensed there was an increased level of activity which was leading up to something big and they felt that they were part of it.

With the increase in army traffic, travelling on the narrow roads around the village had become hazardous and there had been several collisions involving army and local traffic. It was PC Harper's considered opinion that, if things carried on at this rate, there'd soon be no cars left in the village at all. Unfortunately, two accidents had involved local children on bikes and so Harper had visited the village school to warn the pupils of these new dangers.

When Ali cycled to work, she was relieved that she didn't encounter any problems. Three days had passed since her meeting with Peter Pritchard – three frustrating days because she'd been asked by Dr Madely to help rearrange some dormitory furniture and this had prevented any progress on searching the remaining staff bedrooms. And today, Thursday, was the last day before the girls departed for their extra holiday.

Arriving at Lynton House, she immediately gathered her cleaning materials and headed upstairs to resume her duties and to continue her search.

She decided to start with Christine Edwards' room but, when she knocked on the door, she was surprised to hear a croaky voice which invited her to enter. Chris Edwards lay in bed, clearly suffering from a heavy cold.

"Good morning, Miss Edwards. I didn't expect to find you in. You sound as though you need the doctor," she said with concern and puffed up her pillows while Chris Edwards leant forward, before she lay back again in greater comfort.

"Thank you, Miss Jenkins," she said, weakly. "That's very kind."

"Nonsense," she replied brightly. "Is there anything that you need that I can get for you?"

"No, no thanks. Dr Sayers came last night and gave me some disgusting stuff to take. Makes me feel really woozy," she wheezed. She then frowned with concentration and tried to sit up.

"There was something I needed to tell you, wasn't there...? Something about Cheltenham and staff bedrooms," she rambled weakly.

Ali tensed with expectation.

"But this medicine is so strong I can't even think straight. I'm sorry. All I want to do is sleep." She flopped back on her pillow again and closed her eyes.

Ali managed to conceal her disappointment.

"Don't worry about that," Ali told her. "You just concentrate on getting better. I won't do your room now. You need some peace and quiet, but I'll look in on you later on to see how you are." Ali tiptoed to the door and closed it quietly behind her.

It occurred to Ali to check Mr Gloyne's room again to see if the package was still secured under his dressing table drawer. Climbing the stairs, she walked more casually than she actually felt along the creaking landing to Gloyne's door and knocked. As she anticipated, there was no reply so she unlocked the door and went straight to the dressing table. She knelt down and felt along the underside of the drawer. She could feel nothing! She felt again, but still felt nothing.

She bent down and looked underneath. The package had gone!

She froze momentarily as a wave of alarm went through her. This could only mean one of two things. Either the spy had managed to search each of the rooms until he or she had found the dressing table and had retrieved the package – or Gloyne had discovered what was restricting the movement of his drawer and had removed the package, although this seemed to Ali most unlikely.

"Oh, bugger and bloody hell!" thought Ali aloud, not one usually given to swearing. All her previous confidence that they were one step ahead of the enemy evaporated in a moment. Clearly, this was no longer the case. But where could the package be? She had no option but to continue her search of the other staff bedrooms in the hope that she'd be able to find it.

The remaining staff bedrooms were located next to one another in a separate wing, below on the first floor. They were set apart from the pupils' dormitories and were reached by a short corridor which led off the first floor landing.

Ali headed down the stairs and along the landing. The first in the row of four doors in this corridor bore a neat nameplate which announced that this room belonged to "Muriel Phelps BA Cambs.".

She was about to knock on the door when it occurred to her that it would be helpful to know if any of the other rooms were occupied. But a quick check confirmed each room was empty.

However, as an added precaution against any unpleasant surprises, she placed the large tin of Mansion polish on a loose floorboard at the end of the corridor. Here, she removed the lid and balanced it precariously on the tin so that it would fall noisily at the slightest movement. She then trod on the floorboard to check if it worked and the lid fell onto the bare wood with a loud clatter.

Pleased with this result, she rebalanced the lid and paused, listening intently, but the only sounds came from the classrooms below.

Using her pass key, she went into Miss Phelps' room and looked through the drawers and cupboards, taking care to return everything as she found it. Ali hadn't expected to find anything suspicious and she wasn't to be disappointed. There were a few framed photographs on the dressing table, presumably of relatives. Beside them was a small pile of knitting journals. The wardrobe contained a modest collection of clothing and the chest of drawers held an assortment of plain and unexciting ladies' garments, all smelling of mothballs and a set of dentures in a hard, brown cardboard box. Two drawers, however, were full of skeins of navy and khaki wool and knitting needles. On the chair beside the bed was a part-finished knitted sock.

Despite the tension that she felt, Ali smiled. Miss Phelps was obviously "doing her bit" for the War effort.

Ali quickly cleaned the surfaces before leaving the room and locking the door behind her.

"One down, three to go!" she thought.

The next room belonged to Roger Jones. She unlocked the door and went in. As she expected, his room was as tidy as on all the previous occasions that she had cleaned it. She glanced around her. There were the usual exercise books in neat piles on his desk and the small book case contained volumes of geography textbooks, various atlases and reference books on climate and geology. A number of framed photos featured families and friends and there was one of a younger Mr Jones standing proudly beside a biplane.

Ali turned her attention to a small, polished, metal box, placed precisely in the centre of the dressing table. She prised open the tightfitting lid but found it was only filled with an assorted collection of collar studs, tiepins and cufflinks.

Next, Ali carefully went through the contents of his drawers, meticulously replacing each of his garments as she had found them. She then turned her attention to his wardrobe, which contained several suits and an overcoat. She checked each of the pockets but found nothing more suspicious than an old cinema ticket and a receipt for shoe repairs, dated 1940. In view of her experience in Mr Gloyne's room, she then felt along under the drawers for anything which could be hidden there. There was nothing.

As Ali was cleaning, it struck her that this was a very neat room. Everything was in its place, the bed was well made and the clothes were precisely folded. Even in Miss Phelps' room (and she was a stickler for tidiness) there were a few things which were slightly out of place. Here, in Roger Jones' room, there was an orderliness which seemed almost too good to be true. If only the other members of staff were as tidy!

The next room along the corridor belonged to Alice Clarke. Although similar in size to the others, it had an altogether more homely appearance. The curtains were coloured and several framed colour prints adorned the walls. There were also a number of framed sepia photographs of sports teams of a previous era. Closer examination revealed a very young Alice Clarke as proud captain of her teams at St Mary's College. The carpet piece in the centre of the floor, which was clearly not "school issue", helped to soften the functional surroundings.

Miss Clarke had clearly led an active life and, from the group photo of her with a party of students posing on Sydney Harbour Bridge, Ali concluded she was also well travelled. She had certainly succeeded in placing her personal stamp on the room but, as for her being a Nazi spy, a search of her possessions revealed nothing to raise Ali's suspicions and she closed and locked the door.

"Three down, one to go," thought Ali.

Colin Sharples' room was at the end of the corridor and it was the usual untidy mess. On the unmade bed lay an opened paper parcel of clean clothes with a clothes list from the Devizes Clock Steam Laundry and, beside it, a cluster of dirty clothes ready for the wash.

The tops of every piece of furniture were covered with piles of books and papers, except for the bedside cabinet, where there was a small, gilt alarm clock. An impressive brass inkwell and a selection of pens and pencils cluttered the desk surface and, between two bookends, were a number of Chemistry textbooks and a book of logarithmic tables.

Ali cleared away the clothing into drawers and the wardrobe. The dirty linen she left in a pile on the bed, which she had already straightened.

She then began her search, starting as before by checking the bottoms of all the drawers, but there was nothing. She wasn't unduly surprised; she'd somehow discounted Colin Sharples from being mixed up in this business, despite the words of caution she'd received in her briefing from Peter Pritchard.

Ali then checked the wardrobe; nothing unusual there. Next came the chest of drawers where, except for the clothes she'd already put in, she found nothing.

Finally, she turned to the small bedside cabinet, comprising a top drawer above a small cupboard. She began with the cupboard which she found to contain some worn shoe cleaning brushes and an ancient pair of shoe lasts.

The small drawer contained an assortment of items and bric-a-brac which had clearly been thrown in without any thought for tidiness. Amongst these was a bundle of folded paper. Out of curiosity she retrieved the bundle and unfolded it to find an old Chemistry examination paper, a bloodstained envelope and, lastly, a folded sheet of lined paper .

Ali then gasped in shocked surprise when she realised she was holding the missing list of furniture allocations in Hattie Perkins' looping handwriting! Why did Colin Sharples have this in his possession? Surely he can't be mixed up in this, let alone be the Nazi that Peter Pritchard and his team were chasing? Sharples had always seemed such a pleasant person to Ali. She thought of opening the letter but then opted to check the rest of the drawer's contents by pulling it out completely to see what else it contained.

And it was then that Ali got the severest shock. Taped to the back of the drawer was the package that Ali had last seen stuck to the bottom of Gloyne's dressing table. Ali felt her blood run cold. The German passport, the folded papers and the miniature camera… there could be no mistake! They were all there!

"You *bastard*! You absolute *bastard*! How *could* you? How *could* you?" repeated Ali to herself, with a sob almost of anger and disappointment at having trusted this apparently pleasant man.

There was a sudden crash outside and a surprised exclamation. Ali's early warning system had been triggered by someone approaching from the landing. She tried to recover her composure and, with trembling fingers, she quickly shoved the paper bundle into the drawer, before sliding the drawer back into place as quickly and as quietly as possible.

She then busied herself with some dusting. If it was Sharples returning to his room she needed to be behaving normally when he came in. She was then relieved to hear someone unlocking a nearby door and then the sound of a door closing.

Ali was desperately trying to recover from the shock of her discovery and her mind was in turmoil as to what she should do next. Her heart was still thudding and she felt slightly dizzy.

She decided to get out of the room in case Sharples returned so she gathered up her cleaning things and went into the corridor. As she locked the door she became aware of a movement behind her and she whirled round to be greeted by Roger Jones, who was coming out of his room.

"Good morning, Miss Jenkins," he said. "Are you feeling OK? You look rather pale."

"Yes, thank you, Mr Jones," gasped Ali. "I've just had a bit of a shock, that's all."

"And so have I. I nearly collided with that tin of polish you left on the landing."

"I'm so sorry. It was a silly place to leave it," replied Ali shakily. "I was going to polish the landing after I finished your rooms and I left it there, ready to use."

"Well, if you sure you've recovered I must get back to my class," said Jones and turned towards the stairs, while Ali picked up the tin of polish and followed him.

As they reached the stairs, they heard Chris Edwards' croaky voice calling out urgently from along the landing.

"Miss Jenkins! Miss Jenkins! Can you spare a moment? I've just remembered what I had to tell you!"

They both turned round to see Chris Edwards, a blanket pulled round her shoulders, peering out of her door.

"Oh, Miss Edwards. You shouldn't be out of bed," exclaimed Ali. "You go back into your room and I'll come and see you in a moment when I've put my things away."

"Yes, she's right, Chris," agreed Jones. "You must keep in the warm. Is there anything we can get for you?"

"No, thanks, Roger. I just wanted a word with Miss Jenkins."

Chapter Fourteen

At the Roundway intelligence headquarters, the wail of the air raid siren on the roof had slowly subsided to a growl after the daily practice. Staff, all carrying their gas masks and tin hats, returned to their work from the cellars, which now served as an air raid shelter, and the offices around the panelled hall once again echoed to the clatter of typing and the chatter of phone conversations.

Peter Pritchard hung up his tin hat and gas mask behind his office door and checked his watch. He was becoming increasingly concerned that he'd not heard from Ali, partly for personal reasons and partly because, as three days had passed since their last meeting, he'd been hoping to hear news of the results of her searches.

A clerk knocked and entered, carrying several files marked TOP SECRET, which he added to an existing pile on Pritchard's desk. Pritchard nodded his thanks and leant forward to drag the pile in front of him. He was about to open the topmost folder when his red phone gave a loud squawk.

Instinctively, he leant across, grabbed the receiver to his ear and pressed a glowing red button.

"Yes?" he answered brusquely. There was the sound of coins being fed into the call box before the caller pressed button "A".

"Uncle, please," gasped an anxious woman's voice. "This is Apple, Mike, Juliet, two, zero, one."

"This is Uncle speaking. Am I glad to hear from you!" said Pritchard in a relieved tone. "Are you OK? Have you been able to make any progress? "

There was a pause before Ali replied.

"Yes, I'm fine, thanks and yes, I've found our package – but you won't believe where it was hidden!"

Before Pritchard had the chance to ask the obvious question, Ali's excited voice continued. "And there's more! I've got some very interesting information you should know about one of the teachers."

"Then we need to discuss this, but I'm reluctant to do this over the phone. Could you make a meeting in thirty minutes?"

"Yes, I've finished for the day, now. Where shall I see you?"

Pritchard paused. "For obvious reasons, I don't want us to be seen together. Do you know the chalk pit in the plantation near West End? That would give us good cover."

"I'll see you there in half an hour," she said and replaced the receiver. She calculated she'd just have time to get home and make her mother comfortable before cycling back to the rendezvous.

When Pritchard drove into the chalk pit he was relieved to see that Ali was already waiting there. He opened the car door and she clambered in, her shoes caked white from the floor of the quarry.

"Sorry about the mess," she apologised, looking at the chalk on the car floor.

"Sod the mess," he said, reaching out for her and pulling her to him and kissing her hard. "God, I've missed you! Are you sure you're OK?" She smelt cold and fresh.

Ali eased out of his embrace and leant back against the car door, smiling teasingly at him. "Well, look at you. I've only been away for a couple of days and you've already become a gibbering wreck!"

"It's been three and a half days, actually," he corrected her seriously. "When you didn't report in I was worried that something had happened to you."

"Oh, I'm sorry," she replied contritely. "I was just relieved we've traced the package. I hadn't given a thought to how you might be affected when you didn't hear from me."

"No, I'm the one who should be sorry," replied Pritchard. "I didn't mean it to come out like that. You've been the one that's been taking all the risks and I'd become impatient for results. But, go on! Where did you find the package?"

Ali recounted in detail how she had searched the staff bedrooms, how she had discovered that the package had disappeared from Gloyne's room and how she had eventually found it attached to the drawer in Sharples' room, together with the furniture list prepared by Hattie Perkins.

"So Sharples has the package. Well, well, well!" he said reflectively.

"Yes – and he's always been such a nice man. I'd never have suspected him of being a Nazi spy." Ali shuddered. "This certainly bears out what you were saying about trusting no one. So I suppose that all we have to do now is to keep our eye on him and arrest him when he tries to make a run for it."

Ali paused. "And, oh yes. I've been told that it was Sharples who was seen slipping into Kymer's room last week when everyone was at breakfast. So that just confirms he's our man!"

Pritchard didn't reply at first but gazed ahead of him in thought.

"Perhaps, perhaps," he said slowly, still gazing ahead. Then he turned to Ali.

"How certain are you that no one suspects what you've been doing?"

"That's difficult to say. I've always tried to act normally, so I don't think I've aroused anyone's suspicions."

"That's good. But, please remember what I said to you before all this started. Trust no one – even now that we know where the package is."

Ali was surprised at Pritchard's urgent tone of voice.

"But, surely that clears everything up. We know where the threat lies so all we need to do is keep our eyes on Sharples."

Abruptly, Pritchard grasped Ali's arms so firmly that it made her gasp.

"Ali! Please listen to what I'm saying! Things aren't always as simple and as clear cut as they appear to be. It is still crucial that you stay cautious because, if anyone knew – or even suspected – that you have this vital information, your life could be in danger. Promise me that you'll be extremely careful."

He released his grip on her arms and Ali sat back, shocked at the intensity of his warning.

"Don't worry. I promise I'll be careful."

"Good. Now what's this about a member of staff?"

She paused for a moment. "Well, there is one teacher, Chris Edwards, who confides in me because she thinks I'm an ally."

"Oh, and what have you done to make her think that?" Pritchard asked.

"Well, I've got to know her quite well because I clean up her art room, which is always left in a dreadful mess by her classes. She feels guilty about me having to clear up after her and that's when she'll sometimes come and confide in me about things going on in the school. It was she that saw Sharples going into Kymer's room."

"What else did she tell you that could be so interesting to us?" asked Pritchard.

"Well, it's about this man, Richard Kymer. You remember, he's the one who arrived at the school at the same time as Chris Edwards. Well, when he was introduced to the other staff, he gave them to understand that he'd previously been teaching at the Cheltenham Ladies' College for the past seven years."

"So what's so interesting in that?"

"Initially, nothing at all – except that Chris Edwards was a little puzzled why an established teacher should leave such a prestigious job after seven years to come and teach in a small private school in a Wiltshire village."

Pritchard interrupted. "That does sound unusual, I grant you, but there could be a dozen explanations why he wanted to move to St Hilda's."

"Ah!" continued Ali. "But he had bargained without meeting Chris Edwards. You see, Chris had also previously taught in Cheltenham, so she knows the area well. And what's more," Ali paused for effect, "Chris has a friend who still teaches at the Ladies' College."

"I still don't see why Kymer should be under any suspicion," objected Pritchard, "merely because this Chris Edwards woman has these connections."

"Oh, it gets much more interesting," Ali continued, excitedly. "Chris had pricked up her ears when she first heard Kymer mention Cheltenham and she got chatting to him, without divulging details of her own connections there. And during the course of their conversation he said something which really rang alarm bells. He said he was a keen walker and he'd said he enjoyed looking northwards from the top of Cleeve Hill – that's a local landmark – and seeing the town spread out below him."

"OK. So he likes rambling. There's nothing unusual in that."

"Yes," Ali continued, "but Cheltenham lies to the *south* of Cleeve Hill, not the north! So the initial reservations that Chris Edwards had had about Kymer's story appeared to have some substance."

"Yes, but he may just have got his bearings mixed up," objected Pritchard.

"Not on such a basic fact, surely? Anyway, Chris Edwards wasn't convinced and so she phoned her friend at the Ladies' College. And, guess what! Her friend was able to confirm that no Richard Kymer, nor anyone with a similar name or description, had ever been near the place!" Ali concluded triumphantly.

"Oh, and there was something else," she continued, "Chris Edwards is pretty certain Kymer is having a steamy affair with Dawn Crosby – although that may not have anything to do with this business."

Pritchard paused as he absorbed Ali's story. "Right. So, at this stage, all we can say is that this man, Kymer, is not all that he says he is. Mind you, it won't be the first time someone's falsified their references to get a job… or had an affair with an attractive colleague."

Ali looked disappointed. "But," she protested, "he's consistently lied to cover himself. He also reckons he was invalided out of the army, and I bet that's all nonsense, too!"

She paused before adding, "Gosh! I've just had a thought. P'raps Dr Madely is involved in this in some way as well. After all, she'd surely have learnt that Kymer hadn't taught at Cheltenham when she followed up his references. And remember, it was she who told the staff where he'd come from. They have all assumed she's telling the truth – all, that is, except Chris Edwards."

"You could be right about Madely, of course, but I think that's very unlikely," said Pritchard. "Look at it this way. Since the start of the War she's probably been struggling to get staff and, when Kymer comes along with his shining application, she can't believe her luck. After all, it wouldn't be too difficult for him to forge glowing references on the right headed paper. And you'd expect him to have a story to cover his tracks."

"Yes, but that still doesn't explain about Kymer's background or where he's come from… or what he's up to now."

"You leave Kymer to me. I've some military contacts that'll be able to confirm if Kymer was ever at Catterick," said Pritchard. "They'll also be able to tell me if anyone of that name was invalided out. In the meantime, you take the utmost care."

Pritchard paused. "D'you know if the Edwards woman has talked to anyone else about her suspicions regarding Kymer?"

"No, I don't think so," replied Ali, "although I couldn't be sure about that."

"What about when she was confiding in you. Could anyone have overheard that conversation? Did anyone else know she even wanted to speak to you?"

It was Ali's turn to pause in recollection. "Yes, Mr Jones was with me on the landing when Chris asked to speak to me, but I don't think he was particularly interested. In any case he went downstairs ahead of me. And he wasn't around when I went back up to have my chat with Chris."

"Right, I see." He turned to face Ali. "Now it's vital that these developments don't change how you react in your dealings with anyone at Lynton House. Continue to act normally and keep your eyes peeled."

"Oh, I will, don't worry. Anyway, most of the girls will be leaving tomorrow for their special break, so I'll be busy in the morning, clearing up the dormitories after they've left. Then I promised the vicar that I'd help at the village school in the afternoon to prepare for the Spitfire party on Saturday."

Pritchard smiled for the first time since their meeting. "Crikey, you've taken on a lot. Mind you, I expect the party will be fun – and all for a good cause, too."

"It *will* be fun. We *need* to have some enjoyment. God only knows we have little enough of it at the moment." She paused and suddenly said, "Why don't you come? It'd be a good excuse for us to meet in public."

"What a good idea. I'd love that and I'd have my first chance to see you dolled up in your party finery. Now that's a sight I can hardly wait to see."

"It starts at seven, so don't be late or I might find one of those attractive men from the American camp to keep me company!"

Pritchard laughed. "Don't worry. I'll be there on time. I'd hate to find you in the clutches of some American cousin!" he said, and leant over to kiss her goodbye.

Chapter Fifteen

At the village school, caretaker Ron Mortimer had pushed back the heavy dividing screen between the two senior classrooms and cleared the desks away to reveal the full extent of the hall floor.

Ali had joined the army of volunteers from the village and they began to transform the school room into a party hall and now it was festooned with handmade bunting, paper chains and streamers. Several union Jacks hung from the walls while, on one wall, there hung a "Wings for Victory" poster.

Outside, the heat of the afternoon sun beat down and, despite the school's widows being fully opened, everyone found it was hot work.

A large, framed photograph of King George looked down on proceedings from the wall above the coke stove, which was surrounded by its heavy metal fireguard. In pride of place, a very large cardboard cut-out of a Spitfire, painted in camouflage colours and complete with RAF roundels, hung from the ceiling. On the nose cowling was printed "A gift to the RAF from the people of Barton Cannings".

Some trestle tables were placed at one end of the hall, ready for the refreshments and, at the other end, chairs and music stands were set up in front of Phyllis Ponting's basic drum kit, ready for the band. Around the hall were placed chairs which had been borrowed from the American camp and, at last, everything was ready for the party on the following night.

The first to arrive at the school was the Rumain family. Each of the five children carried trays and dishes of delicious, home-made cakes, pies and turnovers, which they arranged on the trestle tables. Bessie Rumain's reputation in the village for her mouth-watering produce was entirely justified, despite the strict rationing, and her rhubarb tarts, apple flans and gooseberry turn-overs were legendary.

These offerings were soon joined by jam tarts, cheese straws, sandwiches of every description and jugs of fruit squash, all brought by a seemingly unending queue of villagers, as the hall rapidly began to fill.

Headmaster Barry Dyke was amazed at the numbers of supporters streaming in past Wallace Macintyre, who collected a two shillings admission from adults and thruppence from each child.

All the women and girls were wearing their best party dresses, some more revealing than others, while many of the men wore their best suits and some had their hair slicked down with brylcreem in styles they'd seen at the cinema. Even the Scanton brothers had come looking presentable and Corporal Caleb Berkley and some American soldiers, in smart uniforms, had come from the US army hospital. The numbers were swelled still further by a number of RAF personnel and soldiers from Devizes.

Constable Harper stood self-consciously next to the Reverend Blunt, who'd secured a place by the coke stove. Harper felt uncomfortably conspicuous in his uniform in all this revelry, even without his helmet, which Phyllis Ponting had taken from him and placed on the mantelpiece.

The band struck up and the hubbub of excited conversations in the hall increased in volume as the villagers began to relax into a party mood. Couples immediately took to the floor and started an energetic quickstep while the older boys stood shyly at the side. From here they watched, fascinated by the bouncing bosoms and the expanses of thigh being revealed by the uninhibited whirling of the younger women.

In all this excitement it was easy for Peter Pritchard to arrive inconspicuously. He squeezed into the hall where he stood in the cluster of people by the door and immediately looked for Ali in the crush of dancers and spectators. Eventually, he saw her dancing with a soldier and, when the music finished, Pritchard broke out from the group and headed towards her through the mass of bodies.

The band struck up with a waltz just as he reached her.

"Would you like to dance, miss?" he asked, tapping her on the shoulder. "My name's Peter."

Ali whirled round in pleasant surprise. "Thank you, Peter. I'm Ali and I'd be very pleased to dance."

Peter led her onto the floor.

"That went rather smoothly," said Peter quietly after they'd been dancing for a few minutes. "I don't think our meeting looked anything other than casual to any possible interested parties."

"Yes," Ali agreed, "but to be sure we create the right impression, I think we should still dance with other people to start off with. We can meet up again during the interval with our refreshments."

Peter fell in with this plan and they made a point of going their separate ways during the dances and party games which filled the next hour.

Barry Dyke was interested to see that Caleb Berkley was apparently being welcomed into the party. He'd not been too sure how the villagers would react to his presence. He was, after all, the only black man in the room and he was the only man taller than PC Harper and, for most of the villagers, this would have been their first experience of meeting this black giant.

A few had, of course, been grateful to Caleb and his team for their help on the day of the plane crash, but the majority hadn't seen him before. So it was opportune that, soon after his arrival, one of the paper streamers became detached from the wall and it dropped on the heads of the dancers, who squealed with surprise and disappointment.

Without waiting, Caleb quickly stepped forward and grabbed the streamer, holding it aloft on his long arm, which only served to emphasise his immense height, before re-fixing the streamer to the wall. Everyone clapped and cheered and, from that moment on, Caleb became an accepted member of the party. When he danced, his body movements to the music seemed different to the local men and this made him very popular with the younger women, who wanted to learn about the new American dances they'd heard on the radio.

As the evening progressed, the hall temperature rose – due partly to the warm evening, partly the exertions of the dancers and partly because the coke stove was now glowing cherry red, thanks to Ron Mortimer's earlier (and unnecessary) stoking. As 'protectors' of the stove, the Reverend Blunt and PC Harper had initially enjoyed their position. But even the metal guard which surrounded the stove was now uncomfortably hot so they eased themselves away to a cooler place beside the door to the cloakroom.

The interval was announced by Arthur Kemp, who'd assumed the role of master of ceremonies and Ali and Peter joined the queue which had quickly formed for refreshments, headed by a number of children.

With filled plates, everyone found somewhere to sit to enjoy their food and the noise in the room diminished as they all tucked in. After a few minutes of relative quiet, Reverend Blunt rapped on an empty milk bottle for everyone's attention.

"Ladies and gentlemen, boys and girls. I know you don't want to hear any speech from me. But there are a number of important announcements that I have to make."

The hall fell almost silent, broken only by the occasional rattle of crockery and cutlery.

"Firstly, I know you will want me to thank, on your behalf, Bessie Rumain and her many helpers for producing such wonderful refreshments for us all to enjoy." He looked appreciatively to where Bessie stood, a beaming smile on her face. "We all know these are hard times and, with all the strict rationing, I don't quite how you managed to do this."

"It must be a miracle, Vicar!" someone called out and everyone laughed, while Reverend Blunt smiled.

"Well, yes, there may be some truth in that. Anyway, ladies, please accept our sincere thanks for all your efforts."

With plates balanced awkwardly on knees, everyone joined in with the applause

Reverend Blunt went on to thank Barry Dyke and his staff for accommodating the party (more clapping) and then it was the turn to thank the band, which received wild applause.

"And now for the most important news you all want to hear." He paused for effect, and silence settled on the room.

"Thanks to all of your efforts over the past weeks and for your donations tonight, the Spitfire Committee is proud to announce you have raised the magnificent sum of..." again, he paused for effect, "eight hundred and fifty-six pounds, seventeen shillings and four pence!"

The room erupted in wild celebration. People clapped, whistled, shouted and hugged each other in celebration. When the din died down, the vicar continued.

"I'm pleased to welcome Squadron Leader Turner, who has very kindly come from RAF Upavon tonight to receive our contribution." He turned to the officer, shook his hand and handed him a large brown envelope.

"Thank you, Reverend Blunt, for that introduction."

Squadron Leader Turner held up the envelope for all to see.

"This is the result of a huge effort and is a truly remarkable sum from such a small village," he beamed. "As you may know, I coordinate the Spitfire Fund in Wiltshire and you'll be pleased to know that this sum will mean we now have enough to pay for another new Spitfire – so Gerry had better watch out!"

The room erupted again with cheering, in which Peter and Ali joined.

"I am meeting with Lord Beaverbrook next week and I shall be sure to let him know that Wiltshire is doing its bit. So, congratulations to you all for such a splendid contribution to the War effort."

After more rapturous applause, people finished their refreshments and the band prepared to start the second half of the evening's entertainment.

Meanwhile, at Lynton House, the place was in virtual darkness and eerily quiet, following the girls' departure. This was accentuated by the occasional creaks throughout the house and the constant moaning of the hot wind which blew warm draughts through the cracks of its many doors and windows.

Somewhere in the house a door slammed noisily, reverberating throughout the building like an explosion, before silence returned.

Christine Edwards was still feverish and recovering from her cold and so remained in bed in her room. She had presumed from the quiet that the building was deserted and so she was slightly alarmed to hear the creaking of the stairs and echoing footsteps on the landing before there was knock on her door.

"Come in," she invited, and the door creaked open to reveal Hattie Perkins, who was carrying a steaming beaker, which she placed on the bedside table.

"There you are, Miss Edwards. I was lucky to get this Ovaltine 'under the counter' from the grocers in Devizes and I thought you'd enjoy some as a nightcap."

Chris Edwards sniffed the Ovaltine appreciatively. "Gosh, thank you, Hattie. What a nice surprise. I didn't expect to see you. I thought that everyone had either gone to the Spitfire party or gone away for the break."

"Lor bless you, no, Miss Edwards. Some of us are still here. I think Mr Kymer was going to the Spitfire party with Miss Crosby and Mr Sharples is still here – and Mr Jones. They're both downstairs in their rooms. I've just taken them both their suppers on a tray."

Chris smiled at Hattie. "Hattie! You really do spoil us. I don't know how you manage it on our coupons. D'you know? With all the shortages and rationing, I haven't had a cup of Ovaltine for nearly two years so I'm really going to enjoy this."

"I thought you'd like it, Miss Edwards. It'll help you to get off to sleep after your nasty cold. Now, if there's nothing else I can get you, I'll leave you to enjoy it and get back down to the kitchen. Good night."

"Good night, Hattie. And thank you again."

When she had finished her drink, Chris Edwards turned down her lamp and lay back on her pillows and was dozing off when there was a tap at her door.

"Come in," she called, opening her eyes. "Oh, it's you," she said, smiling. "Come on in."

The Spitfire party continued well into the evening, with the atmosphere charged by the euphoria of the villagers' success.

Eventually it was time to finish and, after a few more words of thanks from the vicar, everyone stood for the national anthem, which was sung with unabated patriotism, before people reluctantly left for home, hot, tired and very happy – if only for this brief respite from the War.

The night was balmy but very dark night and, since Ali had no torch, she was pleased to accept Peter's offer to walk her back to Lynton House, where she'd left her bicycle. When they arrived they found the house blacked out and, as they opened the side gate, the overhanging trees and shrubs in the grounds made it impossible to see. Peter gripped Ali's hand more tightly as they felt their way along the path at the side of the house and they were about to emerge from the darkest part of the shrubbery when Ali tripped heavily and would have fallen, had

Peter not grabbed her arm. Recovering from this minor shock, they both turned and peered back in the darkness for the cause of Ali's stumble.

At first, it was difficult to penetrate the gloom but, as their eyes became more accustomed, they suddenly froze as they were able to make out the twisted shape of a body, a woman's body, sprawled across the path.

Chapter Sixteen

From the time that Ali made the 999 call at Lynton House, it took nearly an hour for the authorities to respond, although PC Harper had arrived within ten minutes and he took over the protection of the body until Sergeant Bridewell arrived from Devizes with two constables.

"I suppose no one's touched the corpse, Harper?" enquired Bridewell.

"No one, Sarge, except Miss Jenkins. She's the one what found the body when she tripped over it in the dark," Harper replied.

"Was there anyone else with her at the time?"

"No, Sarge. She was on her own. She'd been to a Spitfire party here in the village and she'd come back to the school for her bicycle."

"Where is she now?"

"She's inside, having a hot drink to help her get over the shock," replied Harper, inclining his head towards the building which, due to its effective blackout, was in total darkness.

Bridewell nodded. "I'll need to have a word with her to get her statement. In the meantime, our task is to seal off that path beside the house and make sure no one uses it before the DI gets here from Swindon." He peered at his watch. "He should be here in about twenty minutes, if he's not held up by traffic. And an ambulance is on its way."

He looked across to the double entrance gates and turned to Harper.

"Better get those gates open." He then spoke to his two constables. "Jackson, I want you and Parker to take up places at each end of the path. I don't want anyone blundering through there in the dark and messing up any evidence."

As they took up their positions, an ambulance could be heard in the distance arriving from Devizes, its bell ringing loudly as it progressed around the narrow village roads.

When it finally turned into the entrance gates, its bell still rang out in a deafening clamour. Sergeant Bridewell rushed over to meet it. "Turn off that bloody racket, you idiot!" he yelled at the driver. "D'you want to wake the whole bloody village?" In a quieter tone he directed the driver to park the ambulance to one side of the wide gravel expanse in front of the house and then briefed the crew.

"We have a dead body to retrieve, but we're waiting until the DI turns up from Swindon and also for the doctor to arrive," he explained to the driver. "So there's nothing for you men to do at the moment but wait."

He turned to PC Harper. "Do we know who's in the school building?" he asked.

"I'm not sure, Sarge. When I arrived, Miss Jenkins – she's the one what found the body – she was being comforted by the cook, but I didn't ask if there were any others. But I did recognise that two of the teachers from the school were at the party and I guessed they must have come back some time ago."

Sergeant Bridewell thought for a moment.

"OK, Harper. Come with me and bring your notebook. We need to have a word with those inside."

They mounted the stone steps, knocked on the large door and walked straight into the cool interior without waiting. Inside, Harper closed the door behind them and replaced the blackout curtain. The spacious hall was brightly lit by an ornate oil lamp. This was the first time that either PC Harper or the sergeant had been inside the school and, as they were pausing to take in their surroundings, Hattie Perkins bustled out from one of the adjacent rooms.

"Oh dear, gentlemen. I'm sorry I didn't answer the door. Come on in. You'll be wanting to have a word with Miss Jenkins, I'm sure."

"And who might you be?" demanded Sergeant Bridewell.

"This is Mrs Perkins, Sarge. She's the school cook," said Harper.

"I'm the domestic bursar, if you don't mind," replied Hattie, giving Harper an arch look, "and I've been with Miss Jenkins since she arrived. This is a dreadful business, and no mistake!"

"Yes, well I'd like to speak to Miss Jenkins. But, before I do, can you tell me if there are any other people here in the building?"

"Oh, yes, Sergeant. You see, although Dr Madely and the pupils are all away, some of the teachers stayed in over the weekend."

"How many teachers?"

Hattie paused. "As far as I know there's Mr Jones, Mr Sharples and Miss Edwards – they were all upstairs in their rooms when I last saw them. Then there's Miss Crosby and Mr Kymer. They went to the Spitfire party, but I don't know if they're back yet. Although, looking at the time, I would have thought they should be by now. And then there's two senior girls. They went to the party, too, but I know they're back because I met them upstairs when they came in," She paused. "Oh, yes, there's Miss Phelps. She's just come back from visiting a friend in Bath. And then there's me, making nine altogether."

Throughout Hattie's explanation, PC Harper was noting the details in his book.

"Wouldn't you know if Miss Crosby and Mr Kymer had come in, Mrs Perkins?"

"Goodness, no, Sergeant. In a house this size, and with all the doors we have, it's impossible to know when anyone goes out or comes in." She paused for effect. "Anyway, you'll realise it's none of my business."

"Quite so, Mrs Perkins. Thank you. That's been most helpful. Harper, did you get all of that?"

Harper flapped his notebook shut and nodded. "Yes, Sarge. Shall I go upstairs and check on the whereabouts of the party birds?"

"In a minute, Constable. First I'd like you to be with me when I speak to Miss Jenkins." The Sergeant turned to Hattie Perkins. "Would you take us to her, please?"

Hattie nodded and invited the two policemen to follow her into the room she'd just left. Here, they found Ali Jenkins, sitting on settee, cradling a cup in her hands. Bridewell thought that, for a woman who had just found a dead body, Miss Jenkins looked remarkably composed. Hattie Perkins, on the other hand, appeared very agitated.

Sergeant Bridewell introduced himself. "So you're the young lady who found the body?"

"Yes, Sergeant – although, strictly speaking, I didn't exactly find it. As I told Constable Harper, I just stumbled over it in the dark."

"Do you feel up to answering a few questions?"

Ali nodded. "Yes, of course."

"Right. Firstly, at what time did you find the body, as near as you know?"

"Well, I'd just come back from the party. That finished at around ten o'clock so it must have been at about ten or fifteen minutes after that."

"Why did you come back here? Do you live here?"

"No, I live in Chandler's Lane, but I work here part-time. I'd left my bike here and I came back here from the party to collect it."

PC Harper continued his note-taking as Sergeant Bridewell resumed his questions.

"Did you see anyone in the lane outside, before you reached the school?"

"Yes," replied Ali. "There were a couple of people behind me, but much further back up the lane. I think they'd just come from the party as well."

"Did you see anyone in the grounds," asked the sergeant encouragingly, "either before or after you fell over?"

"No, it was pitch black. I couldn't see a thing... which is why I stumbled over the body."

The sergeant paused again. "I'm sorry to press you on this, Miss Jenkins, but do you have any idea who it was lying on the path?"

"No! I've already told you, it was impossible to see anything."

"Right, thank you, miss. That'll be all for now." He turned to Harper, who nodded his confirmation that the details had all been noted.

He then turned to Hattie Perkins, who had sat beside Ali Jenkins throughout the sergeant's questioning.

"Miss Perkins, has the headmistress been notified of what's happened here?"

"No, not yet," said Hattie. "Things have happened so quickly and I just hadn't got round to phoning her."

Bridewell nodded understandingly. "Don't you worry about that, Mrs Perkins. I'll see that Dr Madely is notified. However, I now need to ask you some questions about what happened here, leading up to when Miss Jenkins arrived."

But Hattie was prevented from any further questioning by the sound of a vehicle turning on the gravel outside and pulling to an abrupt halt, followed by the slamming of car doors.

"That'll be the DI from Swindon," said Bridewell, quickly rising from his chair. "I'll need to continue with your questions after he's given the go-ahead to remove the body. In the meantime, I'd be obliged if you remain in the school. And no one else must leave the building, either."

Bridewell and Harper went out to meet their colleagues.

Detective Inspector Chapman's appearance could be described as unremarkable. He had a rather gaunt and angular frame and draped over it was a creased mackintosh concealing a crumpled suit. Beneath a battered trilby hat, his face gave an expression of having seen it all before. This look of perpetual boredom was tinged with mild annoyance that his evening had been disturbed.

"Right, Bridewell. Where's this body?" he demanded abruptly, without any preliminaries.

"It's on a path over there at the side of the building, sir," he replied.

"Anyone been near it, or touched it?"

"No, sir. Only the woman who stumbled over it."

"When was that?"

"She puts it at around ten fifteen, sir."

DI Chapmen peered at his watch. "So, to our knowledge, the body has been there for at least an hour," He turned to the sergeant. "Has anyone identified who it is?"

"No, sir. I had the path guarded until you arrived in case someone disturbed any possible evidence there may be at the scene," Bridewell explained.

"What about this woman who fell over it? Didn't she recognize who it was?"

"No, sir."

At this point, a car pulled in through the gates and parked behind the ambulance. A plump, balding man got out, carrying a distinctive bag which immediately confirmed his profession.

"Doctor Ingles," he stated, extending his hand to the DI. "Wiltshire Coroner's office. I gather you have an unexplained death on your hands."

DI Chapman made the introductions. "Yes. I'm glad you've got here, Doctor," he said. "We have an, as yet, unidentified body lying on a stone path over there." He nodded towards the shrubbery at the side of the building. "We've been waiting for you to tell us if we can remove it."

"Has anyone touched the body or moved anything at the scene, Inspector?"

"No, Doctor. We've made sure no one's been allowed near it."

"Good. Well, let's go and see what we've got." He produced a torch from his pocket as he started towards the path. "Blackout or not, I'm afraid I'll have to get some light on the scene. Don't worry! I'll only use it sparingly."

Chapman motioned the other officers to follow. "Bridewell, get your man to note down everything."

Harper produced his note book and a small torch in readiness.

Dr Ingles led the way along the path and then paused to turn on his torch to illuminate the body of a woman, clothed in a dressing gown. She was face down in a large pool of blood and her head and limbs lay at grotesquely distorted angles.

The doctor walked slowly round the body, flicking his torch from one place to another before he finally crouched down to make a more detailed examination.

He slowly turned the head to reveal a massive injury to the front of the skull.

"You can see the extent of these injuries. Without doubt, this person died from a compound depressed fracture to the skull. On its own, this would be consistent with receiving a severe blow to the head."

DI Chapman looked at the doctor. "Should we be looking for a weapon of any kind?"

"Oh, there's no need to start a search, Inspector, because I know what killed this woman."

DI Chapman looked marginally less bored at this disclosure. "But you said..."

Dr Ingles smiled. "I was referring to the head wound. If that was the only injury, we could well have been looking for a very large, blunt instrument. However, I also need to take into account the angle of the neck and the attitude of the body and the injuries to the limbs." He pointed to the distorted angles of the arms and legs as the officers looked on.

"The combined injuries would only be sustained by a fall from a considerable height," he explained. At this point everyone looked up the side of the building to where Ingles' torch lit up a second floor window immediately above them. "And my initial guess," continued Ingles, "is that she fell from up there."

He bent down to examine the body more closely. He took some time looking at the head again and then gave an exclamation. Quickly, he diverted his attention to the hands and then the lower limbs.

"Inspector," he said in a sharper tone. "I point out to you two further important injuries."

Chapman bent forward, craning to get a better view of the body.

"Firstly, there is this contusion at the back of the skull. It's above the hairline and I nearly missed it. This is consistent with receiving a blow to the back of the head." He looked up at the ring of faces. "Remember, the other injury to the skull is located at the front."

Ingles then pointed to the marks he'd found on the front of the legs.

"Then there are these contusions on the knees and thighs. They are bruises which are consistent with these limbs having been scraped on a sharp edge."

Ingle stood up. "Inspector, the contusions on the skull and on the legs are important."

"Oh, why's that, Doctor?" asked Chapman.

"They prove that those injuries were sustained while the victim was still alive. Bruises, you see, are caused by ruptured blood vessels which bleed beneath the skin while the heart is still beating."

"So what are you telling us, Doctor Ingles?" Chapman asked.

"Well, I'd prefer to get the body back to the mortuary for a post mortem first, just to confirm my suspicions. But it's my guess that the victim was knocked unconscious before she fell from the window. Now an unconscious person can't just jump out of a window. They'd have to be lifted or pushed out by a third party. In which case, I think you may have a case of murder on your hands!"

The doctor looked up at the window above them. "I'd expect that a detailed examination of that window will confirm my suspicions."

Dr Ingles stood up and turned to Chapmen. "Right, I don't need to see anything else here, so you can remove the body. But I expect you'd like to have the victim identified before we do that?"

Chapmen turned to Bridewell. "Is there anyone in the house who could do this?"

"I expect someone can. If the victim was a resident, I'd expect one of them could tell us who this woman was."

And so PC Harper was dispatched to the house while the ambulance crew retrieved the body. A few minutes later Harper returned, supporting a quaking Hattie Perkins.

"This is Mrs Perkins, sir. She's the domestic bursar here and knows everyone. She's agreed to help us."

Hattie was led across to the ambulance, where one of the crew drew back the blanket, revealing the body.

Hattie reeled back in shock. "Oh, my Lord. Oh, my Lord," she exclaimed.

"Can you identify the body?" asked Chapman bluntly.

"Yes, I can," she wailed. "Oh my Lord."

"Well, who is it, woman?" demanded Chapman, irritably.

Dr Ingles adopted a more friendly approach and placed a supportive arm around her shoulders as he coaxed her. "Now, take your time, Mrs Perkins. Can you tell us who this woman was?"

"Yes, it's Christine Edwards! She teaches..." she paused before continuing. "She was an English teacher here."

At this point, the front door of the school opened and several figures appeared at the top of the steps.

"Go back inside, please," called Sergeant Bridewell, "and remain in the building. We shall be in to see you shortly."

As the ambulance left the scene, followed by Dr Ingles, DI Chapman addressed the sergeant and the four constables.

"Right! I want that room on the second floor secured. No one's to go in there until we've examined the windowsill. And I want statements from everyone in the building. I want details of who they are, where they were between nine o'clock and ten, what they were doing, who they were with and who they saw. I want every detail so make sure I get it! Someone in there is a murderer and I'm going to make damned sure we get them."

Chapter Seventeen

By the time the ambulance left, everyone in the house had come into the common room and, apart from Hattie Perkins, it appeared they had all been in bed when they'd had heard the commotion downstairs.

Hattie had given them a tearful account of identifying the body and the news of Chris Edwards' death had the predictable impact on those in the room; some were sobbing and everyone was speaking at once – partly to comfort Ali and Hattie and partly to express their incredulity, shock and sadness at the sudden loss of one of their colleagues.

Into this scene burst DI Chapman followed by Sergeant Bridewell.

"Quiet, everybody!" Chapman called above the din. The room fell silent.

"I'm Detective Inspector Chapman of the Wiltshire Constabulary and this is my colleague, Sergeant Bridewell."

All eyes were on the two policemen. All, that is, except Ali, who had been watching the faces of the others. If she had been expecting any particular reaction to the police presence, she was to be disappointed.

"As you may already have heard," continued Chapman, "earlier this evening, one of your colleagues, a Miss Christine Edwards, was found dead in the grounds of this house." He glanced around the faces in the room.

This prompted a general murmur of "dreadful" and similar sentiments from the assembled group.

"It looks as though she had an accident and fell from a second floor window and, until that window and the room have been closely examined by a team, which is now on its way from Swindon, no one is to go into it. Do you all understand?"

Everyone nodded and the DI continued.

"In the meantime, I shall be wanting detailed statements from you all on your movements during this evening," and, seeing that Sharples was sidling towards the door, he added, "and, while these are being taken, you will all remain here. Sergeant Bridewell will call you each through to the dining room when it's your turn."

Sharples and Kymer made to protest but Chapman held up his hand. "There will be no exceptions, gentlemen," he insisted. "Everyone stays in this room. And while that's happening, my men will be having a look around upstairs."

"Right," said Sergeant Bridewell, producing a sheet of paper and consulting the list of names provided by Hattie Perkins. "Mr Jones, we'll have you first. Please follow me," and he led the way into the adjoining room.

Chapman then turned to Ali. "Miss Jenkins, since Sergeant Bridewell already has your statement, you are free to leave." Ali was uncomfortably aware that all eyes had now swung in her direction. "But I may want to speak to you again," he added.

Ali nodded her thanks to Chapman and rose to leave the room.

"Will you be OK to cycle home, Ali?" asked Dawn Crosby.

"Thanks, Yes. I'll be fine," she replied as she left the room, closing the door behind her.

Once in the hall she paused to consider her options. Her first thought was to contact Peter Pritchard to confirm that she'd succeeded in protecting his involvement in finding the corpse and to tell him that the body had been identified as that of Christine Edwards.

But, with all the staff now confined to the common room until their statements had been taken, she also recognised the opportunity she now had to re-check the staff bedrooms for any evidence which could identify the Nazi spy.

She instantly decided on the latter course but she realised she had first to convince those in the common room that she'd actually left the building. So she walked to the front door, which she opened and then slammed shut. She then headed across the hall and up the staircase as quickly and as quietly as she could, pausing on the first floor landing to collect a torch from the emergency bag which hung beside the fire extinguisher.

She listened to establish the police whereabouts; the loud clumping of boots above her confirmed they must be in the art room and she guessed that they would be concentrating their attentions up there for some time.

So she turned on her torch and headed for the wing containing the staff bedrooms, removing her master key from her pocket as she went, and stopped at the door to Sharples' room.

She paused momentarily and listed again for any sound of movement. Except for the continuing noises coming from the floor above, there was nothing.

She unlocked the door and went in, closing the door and locking it behind her. She went straight to the bedside table, slid out the drawer and examined the end where the incriminating package had been stowed. The package had gone!

Ali then searched the contents of the drawer for the bundle of papers containing the letter and Hattie Perkins' furniture list. They had gone as well!

Alarmed by her discovery, Ali then made a search of the room in case the items had been hidden elsewhere. To her frustration and annoyance, she found nothing and she was about to leave the room when she heard heavy footsteps approaching along the corridor and then the sound of the door handle to Miss Phelps' room being rattled. Ali quickly turned off her torch and froze, motionless, listening intently.

"This one's locked, Nobby," said a voice.

"I expect they all are," replied another. "We'll need to get the keys if we wants to search this lot. What a damned nuisance."

"Right," said the first voice. "We'd best get back down and tell his nibs. I expect that housekeeper will know where we can get the keys from."

As the sound of heavy footsteps retreated along the corridor, Ali breathed out in relief, glad that they hadn't tried Colin Sharples' door. If that had happened, she would certainly have had some difficulty in explaining her presence – both to the police and, more importantly, to Sharples.

She waited until she was sure that both constables had gone down the staircase before she emerged from Sharples' room and locked the door behind her. As she turned to retrace her way to the landing she heard the sound of approaching footsteps. She'd no opportunity to hide or evade discovery as she saw a shaft of torchlight dancing on the floor and walls, as its holder rapidly came closer and closer. Then, around the corner and into the beam from Ali's torch strode a startled Roger Jones.

"Well, hello, Miss Jenkins," he said, "I didn't expect to find you up here. We all thought you'd left."

While his words didn't actually ask her for an explanation of why she was still in the building and, particularly, in the staffroom corridor, Ali felt that his tone certainly did. But she was just relieved that it wasn't Sharples.

"Hello, Mr Jones. I remembered that I needed to check on the oil levels in the lamps on the landing here before I went home." Then, in attempt to deflect Jones' attention away from herself, she asked, "How did your interview go with the police? I don't know what it is, but that sort of questioning makes me feel nervous, even though I haven't done anything to feel guilty about."

Jones looked serious. "Oh, it was straightforward enough. But, like most of us who were in the house this evening, I was alone in my room. I couldn't prove this and so I don't have an alibi."

He moved past Ali and opened the door to his room.

Turning to Ali, he said, "This is such a dreadful business. And what makes it worse is the police seem to believe that one of us must be the murderer."

Ali was surprised at this response.

"Oh, but I thought the Inspector said it looked like an accident – that Chris Edwards had somehow fallen from the art room window. I didn't hear him say anything about murder."

"Oh, forget I said that. It was just a feeling I had from their questioning." He paused. "Well, in spite of this tragedy, I'm going to try to get some sleep. So, if you'll excuse me, Miss Jenkins, I'll say good night."

"Yes, of course. Good night, Mr Jones." With that, he closed the door, leaving Ali alone on the landing.

She felt stymied by Jones' arrival. She couldn't search the adjacent rooms because he would certainly hear her. She then wondered if there was a chance to check the rooms on the top floor, now that the police appeared to have finished their initial searches in the art room. But she couldn't be sure that they wouldn't return and, furthermore, she'd no way of knowing when Kymer would return to his room on the top floor after his interview with Sergeant Bridewell.

Reluctantly, she went quietly down the carpeted staircase to the hall and, as she passed the common room, she could hear the murmur of conversation as the remaining staff waited to make their statements to the police. She had expected to see at least a policeman or a member of staff as she crossed the hall, but she met no one. She then went down to the basement to collect her belongings, before cycling home.

As she opened the basement door, she was suddenly aware of a movement behind her. The next moment she felt a painful crack on the side of her head. There was a momentary flash of white and then total blackness.

Chapter Eighteen.

PC Harper slumped heavily into his chair in his hot office and gave a weary sigh. It was two thirty in the morning and the long night of police work wasn't quite over yet as he now had to write out his report on the events at Lynton House.

He wiped his brow and then, carefully arranging the blank report forms and his notebook in front of him, he took his pen from his pocket and opened a bottle of ink. He was about to dip his pen nib into the bottle when the phone in front of him rang stridently.

"Bugger!" he exclaimed, glancing up at the clock. Who in hell's name could be calling him at this time? He pulled the phone towards him and lifted the earpiece from its hook and answered. It was Reverend Blunt.

"Hello, Constable Harper. It's Blunt here. I'm calling from the vicarage. I'm so sorry to trouble you at this time of the morning."

"Yes, Vicar. How can I help?"

"Well, I'm extremely worried about Alison Jenkins. You see, I'd been keeping Mrs Jenkins company until her daughter came back from the Spitfire party. But she hasn't come home. She should have been home by eleven o'clock, but she still hasn't arrived. I've left her with Mrs

Stevens while I came to phone you. It's all very worrying for everyone."

"Yes, Vicar, I can see that." As he answered he was thinking of the happenings at Lynton House and he didn't want to cause any alarm for Reverend Blunt or for Mrs Jenkins by divulging any details of Ali's involvement. "Are you sure she didn't arrange to stay with someone else?"

"Oh, no. That's out of the question. You see, she always tells Mrs Jenkins if she has reason to be away and, tonight, she said nothing to her mother about that. In fact, she told her she'd definitely be home before eleven."

"Right, Vicar. Leave this with me and I'll make some enquiries. Don't you worry. I'm sure there'll be a simple explanation for what's happened," Harper replied. "And if I hear of anything, I'll be sure to let you know immediately."

"Oh, thank you, Mr Harper. That's most reassuring. I do hope you'll be able to get to the bottom of this. Good night."

Harper replaced the earpiece on its hook and scratched his stubbly chin. He then lifted the ear piece again and dialled the number of Devizes police station.

When Ali opened her eyes, she could see nothing. All was blackness, although she sensed flashing lights behind her eyes. She was aware of a throbbing pain in her head and of a pungent, musty smell and there was an unpleasant taste of something thrust in her mouth. When she eventually made a tentative effort to move, she found that she couldn't.

Slowly, Ali began to recover her senses. Beside a thumping headache, she felt nauseous, with a stinging taste of vomit at the back of her throat. She gradually became aware that some kind of hood was pulled over her head and, after further attempts to move, she realised she was tied to a chair and her arms and legs were totally numb.

She tried to suppress a rising feeling of panic and, through the waves of increasing consciousness, questions flashed through her mind. Where was she? How long had she been there? Who could have done this to her and what did they want?

She renewed her attempts to free herself but, although the chair creaked noisily, the ropes which bound her were tied securely and the exertion made her head throb unbearably. It felt very warm and she was sweating freely, although this was partly due to her state of shock and to her exertions. Then a spasm of cramp shot through her legs. The pain was excruciating and she tried to scream, but the cloth thrust in her mouth prevented the escape of any sound. Eventually, the cramp and pain subsided and Ali tried to relax her body.

She then realised that one faculty which wasn't impaired by her confinement was her hearing and she listened intently for any sounds which might give a clue to where she was being held prisoner.

At first, all she could hear was her heartbeat thudding in her ears and her snorting breath in her nostrils. Then there was the far-off sound of a door slamming. It was faint and muffled, but there was a familiarity about it and Ali was convinced she must still be somewhere in Lynton House.

Then, she became aware of the sound of shuffling footsteps of people moving about above her head and what sounded like the faint clatter of cooking utensils. If that was the kitchen, she thought, then she must be in one of the cellars in the basement, which was immediately below.

Ali knew the cellars at the house were located next to the boiler room and the small basement room which she used to change her clothes and she vaguely recalled she had gone there after the police had called.

Oh, yes... the police, she recalled hazily. Then, in a sudden tumbling rush, the events of the previous evening came flooding back.

At the Roundway intelligence headquarters, Commander Peter Pritchard had been waiting impatiently for news from Ali. On his return from Lynton House, he'd tried to get some sleep on the camp bed in his office, but he'd only grabbed a few minutes of fitful rest. He eventually gave up and he now sat at his desk, poised in readiness for any information on the developments of the previous evening. So, when his red phone gave a squawk, he instantly leant forward and snatched it to his ear and listened intently.

Ali had lost all count of time in her concussed state. Her body had suffered several more spasms as her bindings prevented any movement and she drifted in and out of consciousness, awaking each time to the pain in her arms and legs.

Then there came the sound of the basement door being opened and, moments later, the door to the cellar was being unlocked. Relief flooded through her. At last, someone was coming to her rescue.

She became conscious of someone standing beside her, but this person gave no exclamation of pleasure or surprise at having discovered her. Instead, they bent forward and whispered hoarsely in her ear. It was a man's voice, strangely devoid of any emotion.

"So, you're awake, now." There was a short pause. "That is good, because you are going to tell me what you know about certain possessions of mine."

Ali inwardly recoiled in panic and suddenly felt very cold. She tried to turn her head away from this menacing voice but her bindings limited any movement. Her mind was racing. Who was this man who talked in whispers?

The whisperer continued but, this time, in a low voice which Ali still failed to recognise. "You see, these items are very important to me and I must have them back immediately. So you will tell me where they are."

Ali could only resort to shaking her head and trying to scream, but this only made her feel dizzy and the only sound she gave out was a high-pitched moan through her gag.

There was a short pause, and then her visitor continued in the same flat intonation which made his words the more menacing.

"If you tell me what I want to know, no one will be hurt. But if you're obstinate, like that foolish Edwards woman, then I may have to resort to physical harm... and your mother is such a frail lady, isn't she?"

Ali froze in horror. Up to this point, she'd only been concerned for her own safety. How could this man possible know her mother?

"Oh, that surprises you, does it?" her captor continued. "Yes, I know all about your mother. Such a charming lady. Very trusting, but a little gullible, wouldn't you say? And I'm sure she'd welcome me, like all her other visitors. I would read to her like the others but, when it was time for her to take her tablets, I couldn't promise to give her the right ones."

Ali shuddered in horror at the picture being painted by this sinister voice.

"You see, I have a number of tablets which would be lethal, when combined with her existing medication. The cause of her death would be attributed to her taking the wrong tablets in her confused state of mind, typical of an elderly lady."

"You absolute bastard," Ali tried to scream. "You Nazi bastard!" But the only sounds that the gag allowed were an unintelligible shriek.

Again, Ali tried to struggle, but she remained trapped, snorting through her nostrils from her exertions and her head thumping.

There was then a long, silent pause and Ali thought that she was again alone. Then the menacing voice resumed.

"I'm going now, but I'll be back in an hour or two – after I've helped to misdirect the search being organised to find you. While I'm away, just consider the price you would pay for your silence."

Ali heard the cellar door being closed and locked behind her.

Desperately, she tried to dredge up the SOE training she'd had on interrogation methods and the techniques used to resist them, but none of the strategies seemed to fit her present situation.

Escape must be her priority, she decided, but how could she get out of this chair?

Her captor had let slip one bit of information – that she had been declared missing and that a search was already under way to find her. This gave her a faint surge of hope, only then to be snuffed out. Surely, she thought, this would have started with a thorough search of the school buildings and, if so, why hadn't anyone thought to look for her in the cellars?

Her mind wandered randomly around the recent events, with one recollection flowing to another, without any logical sequence. People's faces slid past the window of her mind. There was Peter Pritchard, Reverend Blunt, her mother, Chris Crosby, Constable Harper, Alfie Barter and so many more, all tumbling past her.

When the face of Hattie Perkins came into focus, Ali vaguely recalled snatches of conversations she'd had with Hattie – the slamming of the airing cupboard door that had made her jump, the problems of menus on limited rations, changes to the dormitories, the reshuffle of staff furniture. The furniture!

Ali's mind cleared momentarily. What was it Hattie had said during that conversation? Something about new chairs?

"Come on!" urged Ali to herself. "For God's sake, concentrate!"

Then, suddenly, Ali remembered Hattie saying that the old chairs were riddled with woodworm – "rotten as pears" were her words – and that she'd moved these all to the cellar.

"If that's the case," thought Ali, "I'm probably sitting in one of these old chairs now."

Ali felt a renewed surge of hope. If only she could put her chair under some sort of pressure, perhaps it would be sufficient to break and she might then free herself.

She found that her legs had been bound with her feet flat to the floor and, after a few experimental pushes with her toes, she found she could rock the chair backwards and forwards in a creaking movement.

Given a final thrust, the chair teetered backwards and crashed noisily to the floor. Ali had hunched forward to avoid her head hitting the ground and she'd braced herself for the fall.

She was now lying on her back and she gave some experimental thrusts with her legs and found that one side of the chair had completely shattered. She could now move one leg and one arm and, after further struggling, she succeeded in freeing her right arm completely from her bindings.

Frantically, she clawed off the hood from over her head, tugged away a scarf tied round her face and, only then, could she spit out the foul-tasting rag ball from her mouth.

Panting heavily from her exertions, she lay still and took stock of her surroundings. A dim light penetrated from above through cracks in what appeared to be the shutter over the coal chute and she was now able to make out the outline of a pile of coke and, in one corner, a tumble of old chairs.

After renewed efforts, the rotten wood of the chair disintegrated completely. She was then able to untie the sash cord rope on her other arm and leg which had held her so securely. Then, sweaty and dirty and very shakily, she got to her feet.

Her first thoughts were to protect her mother but she also realised she had somehow to tell Peter Pritchard what had happened. But she could do neither of these without escaping from the cellar and, in this respect, Ali knew she had just two options.

She could go up the stairs and through the house, but she discounted this because it carried the risk of being seen by her captor, whoever he was. She'd also have first to break the lock of the cellar door, which would be noisy and attract attention.

Her other choice was to break open the shutters of the coal chute.

Ali climbed up the pile of coke beneath the chute and, balancing on the fuel, which kept giving way under her weight, she examined the underside of the two doors. She saw that the timber seemed very old and likely to provide little resistance to a determined effort to forcing them open. All she needed was something she could use to lever them apart.

As she slid back down the pile of coke she remembered that her captor was due to return at some stage and she frantically started a fumbling search of the cellar for something to help her.

Eventually, among some garden tools covered in coal dust, she found a rusty spade. Using this, she tried hitting upwards at the doors, but they held fast, despite their dilapidated appearance. Then she found she was able to push the spade through the crack between the two flaps but, when the flaps wouldn't move, she realised that they must be held secure by a bolt on the outside.

Ali moved the spade along the crack until she felt it slide under the bolt and then levered down with all her strength. At first, nothing happened. Then, with a sudden crack, the bolt gave way and she tumbled backwards down the coke pile. Above her, several boards of the shutters had parted and daylight now streamed through the gap into the cellar, momentarily blinding her with its intensity.

She gingerly got back to her feet, blinking as her eyes adjusted to the brightness and, once more, she climbed to the top of the coke pile. She pushed open the two shutters and, by craning her neck, found she was looking across the courtyard at the side of the Lynton House.

Ali grasped the sill of the coal chute and, summoning her final reserves of strength, she pulled herself up out of the cellar and onto the hot flagstone paving of the courtyard, where she lay, exhausted and panting in the sun. She was free!

Chapter Nineteen

Many of the local farmers had been able to take advantage of a sudden and unseasonable heatwave and they were busy getting their bonus of an early hay crop stacked and thatched, ready for the winter. It was becoming oppressively warm and the distant hedges shimmered in the heat haze while, to the east and above the downs, embryo storm clouds had begun to form.

Pritchard ducked involuntarily as a flight of Spitfires roared very low over the hay field, before they vanished beyond some nearby farm buildings in the afternoon sun.

The intensity of military activity was unrelenting and, momentarily, Pritchard reflected on how incongruous it was for the training for the bloody War effort to be imposed on such a rural setting.

He was quickly brought back to reality as the radio crackled in the scout car beside him and the lieutenant handed him the receiver.

"It's for you, sir. She's been found and she's OK!"

"Thank God for that," he exclaimed as he snatched the hot handset and pressed it to his ear. "Yes, this is Pritchard. What's the position?"

He listened intently to the briefing before handing the receiver back to the lieutenant and jumping up onto the vehicle.

"Lieutenant, get me to the Cannings police station as quickly as this heap will take us!"

The Lieutenant grinned. "Yes, sir!" Then he looked down to his sweating driver.

"OK, Jenkins. You heard the commander. Get this thing moving! I want the police station in Chandler's Lane as fast as you can make it!"

Driver Jenkins grinned and wiped his brow. He gunned the engine and, accompanied by much wheel spin and flying turf and hay, the scout car shot out of the field where it had been stationed and skidded onto the Horton road, its whip aerial swaying wildly .

In less than five minutes the vehicle pulled abruptly to a halt outside PC Harper's house, where there were two vehicles already parked, one being a police car. Pritchard leaped down and, instructing the lieutenant to wait, he sprinted up the garden path to Harper's office.

The tiny room was crammed full and stiflingly hot. There was Ali, looking somewhat dishevelled and upset, being comforted by Rose Harper while Dr Sayers was finishing dressing a wound on her head. Meanwhile, PC Harper was making an urgent telephone call under the direction of Sergeant Bridewell, while a perspiring Reverend Blunt watched on anxiously from his cramped corner and dabbed his brow.

Ali rose shakily to her feet and surprised the onlookers when she fell into Pritchard's arms, where she clung on, her breath coming in deep sobs of relief. Pritchard held her tight until she regained some sort of composure and then he gently lowered her into her chair.

"I've such a lot to tell you. You see..." she blurted out, but Pritchard held up his hand.

"Miss Jenkins, that can wait. The important thing is you're now safe. I heard over the radio the gist of what has happened. You've suffered a terrible ordeal and what you need is some rest and quiet, so we need to get you home."

PC Harper was replacing the receiver as Pritchard turned to Sergeant Bridewell.

"I gather there is now a guard on Mrs Jenkins' house?"

"Yes, Commander. As soon as Miss Jenkins, here, gave us her account of what she'd been through and the threat made on her mother, I had a constable call to reassure Mrs Jenkins that her daughter was safe. He's been there ever since with instructions to keep out of sight and to stay there until further notice."

"Well done, Sergeant. Now, for a number of reasons, it's vital that no one – and I mean no one – outside of this room is told what's happened. As far as those looking for Miss Jenkins are concerned, she remains a missing person and the search goes on!"

Although somewhat puzzled by this instruction, everyone nodded their understanding.

Pritchard enquired when the search party was next due to report in.

"They were all asked to re-assemble at five o'clock in the schoolyard for a further briefing," he confirmed, "so that's not for another couple of hours."

"Right," said Pritchard. "Now, Sergeant, if it's OK with you, I'd like to borrow your car for a few minutes."

And so the group broke up, with Pritchard taking Ali home in the police car, having first instructed the lieutenant of the scout car that he should give the appearance of continuing the search, while Reverend Blunt set off for the vicarage on his bicycle.

After an emotional reunion with her mother, Ali eventually took Pritchard into the privacy of the kitchen where she had the opportunity to brief him on the events at Lynton House.

Pritchard listened intently. "So, we now know we're looking for a man. And, from what you heard, this man says he's has been intentionally misleading the search party which is out looking for you. That could prove helpful to us in identifying who this bastard is," said Pritchard. "And we can presume he has some connection with the school. Only an insider could have known about the cellars. But there's been one thing that's been puzzling me! Why weren't you found in the search of the school in the first place?"

He paused for a moment, before getting to his feet. "If you're going to be OK here for a few minutes, I'm going to call in at the school and have a word with Dr Madely."

Ali looked disappointed but said, "Yes, I'll be fine once I've had a good wash and the chance to change out of these clothes. But don't be long, will you?"

He smiled and, giving her a farewell kiss, he went out to the police car.

Dr Madely was a worried woman. She'd just finished a long telephone conversation with her bank manager in which she'd learnt that the school's financial standing was precariously close to being terminal. Added to which she feared that, when some of her parents heard about the recent events at St Hilda's, they may now want to transfer their offspring to other seats of learning which, although having a lesser reputation, had at least managed to steer clear of being a major crime scene.

In addition there was, of course, the need for her to write a personal letter of condolence to Christine Edwards' parents and, on top of that, came the problem of having to appoint a replacement teacher and of reorganising the timetable. Finally, there was the logistical nightmare of getting her pupils back from their extended break.

Although Dr Madely had wanted to cooperate fully with the authorities regarding the death of Christine Edwards and the disappearance of her cleaner – indeed, this had already involved much of her time – she was also anxious that the resumption of the term for her pupils shouldn't be delayed any further. So, when she glanced out of the opened window to see a police car come up the drive and halt outside the main entrance, she was fearful that a yet further visit from the police could only mean more problems and more delays.

So it was with some foreboding that she got up from her desk to answer the front door.

"Dr Madely?" Pritchard beamed, offering his hand. "My name's Pritchard. I'm involved in the search for your Miss Jenkins."

"Oh, yes," replied Dr Madely, accepting Pritchard's hand. "Such a dreadful business. Do you have any news?" As Pritchard had hoped, Dr Madely didn't ask for any proof of identity. She'd presumed only a member of the police force would arrive in a police car.

"Not yet, I'm afraid. We're now following up some new leads and we are still very hopeful that she'll turn up. I just wanted to ask a few more questions about the movements of your staff on the day that Miss Jenkins disappeared."

"Then you'd better come in," said Dr Madely, holding open the door. "We'll go into to my study. We shouldn't be interrupted there"

Pritchard accepted her invitation and followed her into a cool and spacious room. When they were both seated, she looked at him with a puzzled frown. "I must say I'm slightly baffled why you're here because I thought I'd given the other policemen all that I know on that subject. As you will have been told, I only returned last evening, so I can't account for my staff's movements before then. So, how else can I help you?"

Pritchard nodded. "I can understand how you feel, Dr Madely, and I'm very sorry for interrupting your day. My coming here must be very inconvenient for you, I know, so let me make this quick. I just wanted to clarify which members of your staff are helping with the search for Miss Jenkins."

Dr Madely looked impatiently at Pritchard. "But I've already given this information," she said stiffly. "They have all been helping as best they can, although there is a limit to what my older staff can do."

"Yes, quite so," said Pritchard. "Now, although you may not have been here at the time when the searches were instigated, what is your understanding of how each person responded to hearing that Miss Jenkins had disappeared? For example, was there anyone in particular who organised a search of this building?"

"As I've already explained, I understand it was Mr Kymer who first took charge. He allocated a floor to each of the others and they reported back to him after they'd finished their search."

"I see. Now I realise this may be difficult to answer but, from what you heard, do you know who Mr Kymer asked to search which floor? This is very important for us to know."

Dr Madely paused to reflect.

"Well, I gather that Miss Phelps and Miss Clarke took the ground floor. Then Miss Crosby, Mr Jones and Mr Gloyne had the first floor... and Mr Kymer and Mr Sharples, they looked around the top floor."

"I see. And what about the cellars – do you know who checked them?"

Pritchard listened with interest to the name she gave and then he stood up to leave.

"Oh, one final question. Since the search got under way, have any of your staff come back to the school for anything?"

"I think they've all been back at one time or another. That's when Mr Sharples discovered that his room had been ransacked. It was quite extraordinary. Absolutely ransacked! Why anyone should want to do that is quite beyond me. And poor Mr Sharples, he was understandably most upset."

Pritchard looked surprised. "Ransacked, you say. He's reported this to my colleagues, I presume?"

"Yes. But, since nothing appears to be missing, there isn't much they can do."

"I see. Well, thank you, Dr Madely. This has been extremely helpful and I'd be grateful if you wouldn't discuss my visit with anyone for the time being. Now I know you've a lot to attend to and I'm only sorry to have intruded on your time. So I won't hold you up anymore."

Once in the police car, Pritchard headed back to the Jenkins' house, where he found Ali, now spruced up, providing her mother and the police constable guard with tea in the cool of the parlour. When Pritchard came into the room, the constable rose awkwardly to his feet, rattling his cup and saucer and trying to avoid spilling its contents, but Pritchard smiled and waved him back into his chair.

After pleasantries, Pritchard signalled to Ali that she should follow him into the kitchen.

"I've had a word with Dr Madely and, if her information is accurate, I think I know who we are after."

Ali's face hardened with this news. Hoarse with emotion, she asked, "Who is it? I bet it's that Sharples man! I want to know who this Nazi bastard is – this animal who killed Chris Edwards."

Pritchard had not seen Ali in quite such a state before and he also noticed she made no mention of the attack on herself and the threat made on her mother.

"Before I tell you, you should know something else that Dr Madely has just told me."

"Oh? And what's that?"

Pritchard looked across at Ali. "Several members of her staff have been back to Lynton House during the course of their search for you and, when Sharples went back, he found that his room had been ransacked."

Ali momentarily looked puzzled. "Why do you think that's so important? I thought Sharples was our spy. Remember, I told you that he had the package hidden at the back of his drawer."

Pritchard smiled grimly. "Well, Ali, I can now tell you something I wasn't able to share with you before. You see, Colin Sharples was the person I planted at Lynton House!"

"D'you mean he's ..?" started Ali.

"Yes, he's MI6 and a member of my investigating team."

Ali gasped and looked slightly embarrassed. "How could I have been so wrong?" she bemoaned.

"Well, I did warn you that everything may not be as it seems," Pritchard reminded her. "But, most important of all, by the ransacking of Sharples' room we have to assume the spy has recovered his package."

Ali shivered at the recollection of her captivity and the sinister voice which had demanded its whereabouts. "He must have been desperate to retrieve it and, with everyone out of the way searching for me, he must have seized the opportunity to break in to Mr Sharples' room."

Ali paused. "But, why Mr Sharples' room in particular? Why didn't he trash any of the others?"

"My guess is that, once he knew you'd escaped – and remember, only he knew that you'd been imprisoned in the first place – he had to resort to more desperate measures," explained Pritchard. "We know he'd already searched some of the other rooms without success, so probably Sharples' room was next on his list."

Ali suddenly asked, "But what's the connection between this spy and poor Chris Edwards? Why did he have to kill her?"

"I can't be sure at this stage, but I think he suspected that Christine Edwards had stumbled onto something. He may have overheard her say something which led him to conclude – wrongly as it happens – she knew about the package and its whereabouts. In any event, the night of the Spitfire party gave him the opportunity he needed. With the girls and most of the staff all away, he had the run of the building."

Ali shuddered. "Poor Chris. She was heavily sedated with the medicine she was taking for her cold."

"Yes," said Pritchard, "she'd have been in no state to offer any resistance. He may have tried a gentle approach with her in the first place. But when that didn't get the results he hoped for, he turned rough. And once he'd revealed to Christine Edwards his true purpose at Lynton House, he knew he'd have to kill her, whether she had the information he wanted or not. And, unfortunately for him, Edwards only had vague suspicions, but nothing more. So he was still none the wiser."

"So I suppose he overpowered her before pushing her out of the window to make it look like and accident."

Pritchard nodded. "Yes, he was trying to cover his tracks. But then he remembered that Christine Edwards had been particularly friendly with you and he may have concluded that Edwards had confided in you what she suspected."

Ali gasped. "So that's how I ended up tied to a chair in the cellar." She paused and then made a strange sound, her face contorted with a mixture of realisation, anguish and disgust.

"Of course!" she exclaimed. "It's that man, Roger Jones. He's the bastard who killed Chris! He's the bloody Nazi spy!" She sat there, trembling with emotion and Pritchard leant forward to place a consoling arm around her heaving shoulders.

"I've just remembered his room. I always thought his room was too neat and tidy. I should have realised this. No Englishman's room is as orderly as that! God, why didn't I spot the signs?" she sighed.

"This time, Ali, you're absolutely right," he said. "It is Jones. He must have overheard you and Edwards talking at some stage and concluded that you knew about his package. It was just fortunate for you that he had no idea about your real purpose at Lynton House. If he had, I don't think you'd be sitting here now."

Ali shuddered and shook her shoulders as she recalled her ordeal in the cellar. "Looking back, I can see it all, now. There were several occasions when I think he may have overheard us. One was when Chris told me that she'd seen things which made her feel uneasy. Jones came out of the dining room just as she told me that."

She thought for a moment. "It must have been Jones who was trying Mr Gloyne's door when Christine called out that 'he's still downstairs'. Although he was probably able to give a plausible explanation for trying the door, he must have been furious to have been caught in the act by Christine Edwards."

Pritchard nodded. "Yes, and you told me she had later called out to you that she had something important to tell you. Jones was with you then. Remember?"

Ali nodded in recollection. "Mm, and now I think about it, there were others and after linking all these instances together he must have been convinced that Chris knew something. And there was a later occasion – after the arrival of the police, when he caught me snooping on the staff landing. He let slip that Chris had been murdered, while the police were still maintaining they were investigating an accident. I'm sorry, but I should have picked up on that."

Pritchard continued, "Anyway, when Kymer organised a search of the school when you were first declared missing, you can guess who volunteered to search the cellars."

"Jones!" groaned Ali.

"Yes," said Pritchard. "Dr Madely confirmed this when I went to see her. No one else bothered to look there after Jones reported back to Kymer that the cellars were empty. So, no wonder you weren't found! After that, he made sure the searches concentrated on places away from the school." Pritchard gave her shoulders another squeeze. "But he reckoned without the bravery of my Alison Jenkins!"

This made Ali smile for the first time since their reunion, although she then looked puzzled.

"Yes, but now he knows I've escaped, *and* he's got the package. Surely that changes everything."

Pritchard nodded. "It does indeed, and I'm expecting someone to call in here to brief us on the latest developments." Pritchard looked at his watch. "In fact he should have been here a few minutes ago."

As if on cue, there was a knock on the back door and Pritchard walked across to open it.

"Come in," he greeted. "Glad you could both make it." And into the room strode the man she'd been introduced to at Roundway intelligence HQ many months ago as the Controller, followed by Colin Sharples.

Chapter Twenty

The Controller beamed at the gaping Ali and shook her warmly by the hand. "Ah, the resourceful Miss Jenkins! How nice to meet up with you again after all this time." Before she had the opportunity to reply, he inclined his head towards Colin Sharples. "I believe you two know each other."

Pritchard closed the door as Sharples, too, stepped forward and extended his hand to Ali, who was still recovering from the surprise of their arrival. "Yes, of course we do," he said. "Miss Jenkins, glad to see you've returned safe and sound."

"Thank you, Mr Sharples – and I owe you an apology. You see, I was convinced that you were the person we were looking for."

Sharples smiled. "Yes, so Commander Pritchard tells me – and for all the right reasons. Even so, I must congratulate you on what you've achieved. I had no idea you'd been into my room and, from what I heard in the staffroom, no one else knew about your searches either. In fact, your name was never mentioned so you did an excellent job in arousing no suspicions."

At this point the Controller looked across to Ali. "I hope you don't mind our coming into your home like this, only things are moving rapidly and I suggested we meet here to discuss our plan of action."

"You're both most welcome, sir," replied Ali. "Please make yourselves at home. Can I get you something to drink?" She smiled. "There's only tea, I'm afraid, or home-made lemonade."

The offer of tea was accepted and Ali busied herself in producing a steaming mug for everyone. The others found a chair at the kitchen table and sat down.

The Controller looked round the table. "As you all now know, the agent we are after has now been confirmed as one Roger Jones – at least, that's the name he's been using – but I'm confident we'll be able to establish he's a German national with a very different name." He took a sip from his mug and looked across to Pritchard.

"Commander, what's your view on how we should proceed?"

"Well, sir, we have to make a number of assumptions. Colin, here, has been keeping a close eye on him and, from what he reports, I believe Jones will still think he's above suspicion. Remember, he said nothing to Miss Jenkins which could have identified him and, although he knows she's escaped, he doesn't know where she is or who she's spoken to."

Everyone nodded their agreement.

"He certainly won't know the intelligence which we now have and he won't know that we've been able to piece it together to know he's our spy."

"So how should that influence our plan of action?" asked the Controller.

"Initially, I believe we should carry on as though Miss Jenkins is still missing and as though we have no inkling of his complicity," said Pritchard. "This will give us a little time and also, by doing this, Jones is likely to stay in sight as part of the search party and we may be able to manoeuvre him, without arousing his suspicions, into a situation where we can grab him. We should remember he has no reason to stay, now he has his package of information. He's only helping with the search to buy some time, before he tries to leave for the Fatherland. But if we give him the slightest reason to think that his cover is blown, he could just vanish, taking all that information with him."

Pritchard looked at the Controller. "However, we can't spin out Miss Jenkins' disappearance too long and I believe that the moment it's announced that she's been found, that will trigger his move to escape."

Sharples nodded and added, "So we need to give some thought now to how he intends to do that and he only has two options open to him – that's by sea or by air."

The Commander nodded. "Yes, but the sea option seems highly unlikely. He'd first need to travel to the coast, which would take some time, given the state of rail and road transport, with a greater prospect of him being picked up en route. And, even if he was successful in getting that far, he'd still have to get through our very effective coastal fortifications before he could steal a boat. And that's presuming our harbours aren't guarded – which we know they are. And if he'd hoped to be taken off by submarine, then he'll have reckoned without the regular patrols of Coastal Command. No, I believe he's far too clever not to have recognised all of these obstacles."

Sharples nodded. "You're right, sir. I think he's hoping to be picked up by plane. Most grass runways have been ploughed up for food production but there could still be a remote landing strip which he could use. It would be comparatively easy for the Luftwaffe to send over a light aircraft to extract him under cover of darkness."

Pritchard scratched his head. "Yes, but the problem is knowing which one. They might even consider a pick-up from an airfield, although that seems very unlikely."

Ali interrupted. "There is another possibility which you haven't mentioned." All eyes had turned to her. "He might be planning to steal a plane and fly out himself."

"Agreed," said the Controller, "but that presumes firstly that he can fly and, secondly, that he knows from where to steal a plane."

"Oh, I believe he can fly, all right," said Ali. "There was a photo in his room of him proudly standing beside an aeroplane. It was a single-engine biplane and I think it must have been taken at some flying club. From his attitude in the photo, it looked as though the plane belonged to him."

The Commander and Pritchard looked surprised at this information, while Sharples appeared unconvinced.

"But where is he going to find a plane in these times?" he asked. "Anything that's vaguely airworthy has been requisitioned by the War Ministry for pilot training and, as I said, most airstrips have been ploughed up long ago."

There was a short pause, then Pritchard said, "But Miss Jenkins makes an important point. If I were in Jones' position and if I could fly, I'd have been looking out for likely places where a plane might be hidden away." He looked around the others. "*We* wouldn't have been thinking that way because none of us can fly. But he knows what he's looking for and he's had plenty of time to recce the area for likely locations."

Ali joined in. "And there are at least two places locally that I can think of straight away which would suit his purposes." Again, everyone looked to Ali. "The first is at the Horton House estate. Old Colonel Spreadbury used to fly a Tiger Moth there before the War, from his grass runway at the back of the big house. I admit it's a long shot. The plane was mothballed at the outbreak and hasn't flown since."

"On top of which," added the controller, "I doubt if the Colonel has got any fuel, given the present restrictions."

Undeterred, Ali continued, this time her eyes bright with excitement. "OK, maybe that wasn't much help but there's one other place that we all know about that has a plane in working order *and* fuel *and* a grass landing strip in regular use!"

"Good God," exclaimed the Controller, "You mean Captain Masters' place at Baltic!"

Ali nodded.

"You're right, of course," said Sharples, "but would he have the brass neck to do it?"

Pritchard nodded. "Put yourself in his position. He's a desperate man, a fleeing enemy agent who's wanted for murder. Given those circumstances, he'd be desperate enough to try almost anything. My guess is he's aware of the set-up at Baltic, although he may not know about its purpose. I suspect it was Jones that the young Barter boy saw when he was hiding in the hedge that night."

"Well, that would certainly explain a lot," said the Controller. "But taking that plane wouldn't be easy. He'd have to open up the barn, remove the camouflage rigged by Masters' staff, roll the plane out and then start it – all single-handed."

Sharples cut in, "It wouldn't be easy, that's true, but if he's been a flying club member, as Miss Jenkins suggests, none of those would be a major problem for him. And Commander Pritchard is right. He'll certainly be desperate enough to try anything to get out of the country."

"It's a hell of a presumption to make," said the Controller, "but I can't think of any other scenario that fits our intelligence. If we're right, we shall need to move fast to set up a small reception for him. We just can't afford for this bastard to slip through our fingers now." Looking at Pritchard, he asked, "Commander, we'll need some firepower for this operation, which rules out the police. How quickly can you get hold of Brigadier Johnson and Captain Masters?"

"I can get to the police station phone in just a few minutes to set that up. But we also need to think of how we are going to stage manage Miss Jenkins' return so that it has the right effect on Jones as well as on the search party."

Ali finished her tea and put down her mug. "Why don't I wander into the school playground in a dazed state just as the search party is being organised by Constable Harper?" She turned to Pritchard. "My story could be that I must have fallen and hit my head. I don't recall anything and I suffered a number of blackouts. I then eventually regained consciousness and found myself in a ditch somewhere."

Prichard looked admiringly at her. "That's a brilliant suggestion. Would you really be prepared to do that?" Then he added, "To be convincing, I'm afraid it would mean you changing back into the clothes you were wearing before and making yourself look suitably dishevelled – and you'd have to remove that dressing on your head."

Ali looked pleased that her plan might be taken seriously. "Yes, of course I would. I want to see this fiend caught!"

"While that's a commendable suggestion, Miss Jenkins," said the Commander, "I'm concerned on two counts. My first concern is for your safety. We have no way of knowing how Jones will react and I'd want you, Colin, to rejoin the search party when it musters and to be close by to give Miss Jenkins protection, should it be needed."

Sharples nodded.

The Controller checked his watch and then looked at Prichard. "My other concern is timing. If the search party is due to reassemble at seventeen hundred hours, that only gives us a little more than an hour to set up the reception party at Baltic."

He looked at Ali. "So the timing of your arrival at the schoolyard will be critical. If you arrive too soon, Jones could scarper before we're ready for him."

"I appreciate that, sir," said Ali, "so I won't make my appearance until PC Harper's briefing is well under way."

"Jolly good." The Controller nodded, approvingly before turning to Pritchard. "On second thoughts, Commander, to save time it will be best if I speak to Captain Masters myself and alert her to what we're planning. In the meantime, I want you to cut along to the police station and brief PC Harper so that he knows what to expect. Then use his phone and contact Brigadier Johnson to arrange for an armed platoon to throw a wide cordon round the Baltic site." He paused, before saying, "We've a lot to do in a very short time. Good luck, everyone. Let's get cracking!"

When Pritchard reached the police station, he was greeted by PC Harper, who sat open mouthed as he heard the plan to capture the Nazi spy. "Mr Harper, you have a very important role to play. It will be vital to the success of the rest of the exercise that you act as normally as possible at your briefing, you understand?"

PC Harper nodded enthusiastically. This was an exciting departure from his normal duties and he couldn't help feeling just a little smug that none of the senior ranks in Devizes were involved.

"Up to the point when Miss Jenkins arrives, you will impress the members of the search party with your concern that she is still missing after nearly two days of searching. It's important that they are convinced that your concern is genuine – particularly Jones."

PC Harper started to say he fully understood, but Pritchard cut him short.

"And, when Miss Jenkins reaches you, you will take her into your care. Members of the search party will naturally want to talk with her and they'll all want to ask her lots of questions. That's quite understandable but your job will be to prevent this. Dismiss everyone as quickly as possible and take Miss Jenkins to the police station."

PC Harper was absorbing his instructions as Pritchard grabbed the phone and dialled the number for army headquarters at Devizes.

"Commander Pritchard here. I need to speak top priority with Brigadier Johnson. Yes, I'll hold." After a number of clicks and squawks on the line, he was put through.

"Johnson here," answered the brigadier abruptly. "That you Pritchard? How can I help?"

He then listened intently to Pritchard's requests and, to the Commander's relief, his response was immediate and helpful.

"I'll have Lieutenant Jennings contact you toute de suite. An excellent man – he's the platoon commander who's already been detailed to keep an eye on events at Barton Cannings, don't you know. He's familiar with the lie of the land and I understand from his reports that his men are first class, so I've every confidence he'll give you chaps the sort of help you're asking for."

"Thank you, Brigadier. I met Lieutenant Jennings earlier today and so I share your confidence."

Pritchard checked the OS map spread out on Harper's office table and found a location away from the village.

"Would you tell him to meet me in the field behind the Bridge Inn? I don't want his platoon to attract too much attention."

"Yes, fully understood. He'll be there in under five minutes – and good hunting!"

Chapter Twenty-One

The car pulled off the road onto the chalk track beneath the beech trees and, from his rear seat, the Commander could barely make out the two mounds in the long grass on each side of the track made by the heavily camouflaged sentries. He was impressed by Captain Masters' precautions; only a trained eye could have picked them out and then only with difficulty.

As they reached the treeline, they were stopped by two armed sentries, who carefully scrutinised their ID cards, before directing them onwards.

The track led to a yard at the rear of the farm buildings and, here, the car halted in a small cloud of chalk dust beside what appeared to be the door to the farmhouse. A young man in shirtsleeves stepped forward from the house and opened the Commander's door.

"Welcome to Baltic, sir. Captain Masters is expecting you. Please come this way."

The Commander followed him into the cool interior of the house and then into what had once been a large kitchen. On the walls, where once had hung pots and pans and kitchen utensils there now hung maps of all sizes and scales, the largest and most prominent of which was a large scale, detailed map of northern France. Several men and women dressed in civilian clothes were studying the wall maps and making notes and peering through stereo photo viewers at aerial photographs.

A large table filled most of the room and covering the table were more aerial photographs, stereo photo viewers, more maps and numerous documents and papers. Laid over the top of these was a large site map of Baltic farm and its surrounds and poring over its detail was Rosemary Masters in civilian dress. She stood up as the Controller came into the room and walked round the table to meet him. When they shook hands he noticed that, where Masters' hand had previously been heavily bandaged, this had now been replaced by a lighter dressing.

"Captain Masters." He nodded to her hand. "Making good progress, I see."

"Yes, thank you, sir. And welcome to our small abode." She smiled briefly, before pointing across to the plan. "I've been thinking about our task tonight, following your call, and this site plan may help you to understand the layout."

"Thank you Captain. Let's have a look." The Controller walked round the table to where the map lay.

"We already have plans in place for defending this set-up from an attack by alien forces, which may be helpful with tonight's exercise – although what you're asking me to do is to let someone get into the site rather than prevent that happening."

"Yes, I realise that must go against the grain, Captain. But I'm not asking you to let this man just walk into the place. I was thinking more along the lines of making his access easier than he might have anticipated."

"I've been thinking along similar lines. But if I make it look too easy for him, he will certainly be suspicious."

"That's true, of course. So what do you have in mind?"

"Well, presuming he has no interest in the farm complex on this north side of London Road, I'm concentrating our efforts around the barn and the airstrip."

The Controller nodded. "I gather your team will still be securing the farm, though."

"Oh, yes." Masters drew a circle with her finger on the map which encompassed the farm and its various outbuildings. "They'll be deployed around this perimeter, although I doubt if they'll be seen as easily as the two sentries beside the drive."

"Most impressive," said the Controller, who was slightly taken aback. "I presume there's no risk of them being mixed up with Lieutenant Jennings' platoon?"

"None at all, sir. I shall be speaking with him by radio very shortly to detail our positions. He will deploy his men in a much wider circle to take in the whole site on both sides of the road."

"Most impressive," repeated the Controller. He'd always had the highest regard for Rosemary Masters and, now, her calm and professional manner served only to emphasise that his confidence in her was entirely justified.

He pointed on the site map to the barn and the airstrip to the south of the road.

"What about here?" he asked.

"Yes, I've been giving that some thought, sir," she said, looking pointedly at the Controller, "and what I have in mind will hopefully enable you to catch your spy without compromising my continued operation here at Baltic."

"My sentiments, precisely," agreed the Controller. "Our problem is that both outcomes are key to the War effort."

As if to signal to them both that the War was still in progress, four Lancaster bombers roared in formation low over the house before banking away to the south.

Masters looked upwards and listened with a furrowed brow as the roar from their engines quickly died away. "They can't come much lower without hitting our trees," she observed. "Now, to the task in hand. Here's how I intend to deal with the arrival of Mr Jones."

As Pritchard pulled into the field, he saw under the shelter of an overhanging hedge a scout car, a Bren gun carrier and two three-ton Bedford trucks. A number of soldiers stood by the vehicles in a state of readiness, including Lieutenant Jennings, who ran over to meet him.

"Good to see you again, sir. I gather we could see some action tonight."

"Yes," said Pritchard, "although, if everything goes to plan, you shouldn't get involved in any firefight. That will be down to Captain Masters' team."

He looked at the map board that Jennings was holding and pointed to the area occupied by the Baltic holding. "Your task will be to deploy your platoon so that your men completely encircle this area. Under no circumstances must you be seen or do anything to prevent our quarry from reaching this barn, here." He pointed to the barn and airstrip.

"Once he's inside your cordon, no one must be allowed back out until you've been given further orders. There's precious little natural cover, except for this old Roman road to the north and the Wansdyke to the west. There are no hedges up there – just a few bushes dotted about, so your men will need to be well camouflaged."

If Lieutenant Jennings was disappointed at the prospect of no active involvement, he succeeded in concealing it. "Right, sir. My men can be relied on to do that. What time is our bird likely to make an appearance?"

"We can't be certain," answered Pritchard. "Much depends on how things pan out in the village but my guess is he'll make his attempt at around dusk."

"In which case," said Jennings, checking his watch, "we need to get cracking. I'll avoid the village by heading back towards Devizes and then turn back up London Road. With luck, we should be able to tuck in behind a convoy heading towards Marlborough so no one's likely to give us a second glance. It'll add a few minutes onto the trip but we'll still be in position in good time."

"That's good thinking, Lieutenant. I'll leave the details of deployment down to you, but be sure to place your Bren gun carrier at the far end of the runway. In the unlikely event of our man giving us the slip and attempting to take off, you'll have a clear field of fire from there. Under no circumstances must that plane leave the ground! Got that? And be sure to stay in close radio contact. "

"Absolutely, sir." He looked up at the gathering clouds. "Looks as though we could be in for a storm later – in more senses that one!"

Jennings turned and made a circular, whirling motion with his arm to his drivers as he ran to the scout car. The vehicles' engines immediately fired up, the men scrambled aboard the trucks and, in less than a minute, the small convoy had left the field.

Pritchard parked his radio car near the church, removed his jacket and threw it on to the back seat.

Although it was late afternoon, it remained very hot and humid and, looking up at the gathering clouds, Pritchard felt that Jennings' forecast of a storm could well be accurate.

He was forced to wait in his car as a herd of cows, which filled the full width of the dusty road, pushed past him. They were on their way back from milking to their grazing and, to ensure they reached their destination, they were followed by a patient-looking herdsman carrying a milk-can in one hand and a long stick in the other. He knew each of his cows by name and he gave encouraging calls to his charges, accompanied by occasional light taps on their rumps, although he was resigned to their slow, plodding progress.

As the last cow passed, Pritchard got out of the car and walked through the churchyard to the school. There were several villagers ahead of him, going in the same direction, and he correctly guessed they were members of the search party, hurrying back for the five o'clock briefing from PC Harper.

In the school playground around thirty villagers stood in small groups, sharing their concerns about the disappearance of Alison Jenkins. There was Alfie Barter, proudly standing between his brothers, Seth and Henry, talking to the two Scarrott boys. Bessie Rumain was in animated conversation with Phyllis Ponting while Barrie Dyke was discussing matters with Wallace Macintyre and the Reverend Blunt.

By mingling in with the late arrivals, Pritchard was able to join the group without drawing attention to himself and he saw that Sharples was already present and had stationed himself near the entrance to the yard. Pritchard's eyes flicked round the heads until they rested on Martin Kymer, who was talking to Mr Gloyne and Miss Phelps. Then his body stiffened as he saw, in the same group, the back of Roger Jones. The man's audacity made Pritchard momentarily fume.

Pritchard had little time to dwell on those feelings because PC Harper arrived on his bicycle and became the centre of interest as he dismounted, slowly removed his cycle clips and turned to address the gathering.

At that moment a clap of thunder rumbled to the east, causing everyone to look round at the clouds, which were creeping towards the village. A small breeze began to blow, hot across the playground, whipping up dust and paper litter in mini whirlwinds on the tarmac.

PC Harper's voice broke the momentary lapse of attention.

"Thank you all for coming back this afternoon. I know that this is a very distressing time for all of us and I'm sorry to tell you that we have no more news than when I spoke to you last time. I was disappointed to hear some talk that hopes must be fading of finding Ali Jenkins alive." This was greeted with murmurs of shock and concern.

Harper held up his hand for quiet. "However, I'm convinced that she's still out there somewhere and it remains our job to find her. Now, I need to change the areas of search and, if you'd kindly pay attention, I'll divide you up into teams again." He produced a map of the village and he was just showing where the first team should begin its search when someone at the back shouted and pointed, "She's here! She's here!"

Everyone turned to see Ali swaying across the playground, looking dazed and dishevelled. Pritchard mentally gave her an award, both for her timing and for her convincing performance, while Sharples and Harper showed equally convincing concern and rushed to support her.

Pritchard watched as there was a momentary pause, when the expressions on the faces of the gathering quickly changed from shock to relief and then to joy at Ali's safe return. Then, suddenly, everyone moved at once. People wanted to speak to her, touch her, sympathise with her, hug her, listen to her, resulting in a melee of bodies and a cacophony of sound as they all converged towards her and, if it hadn't been for the timely intervention of the two men, Ali would have been swamped under a human tide of kindness and welcomes.

Harper raised his hand in an appeal for order. "Stand back, now. Please give her some room." As the crowd fell back, he and Harper lifted Ali between them and headed towards the playground entrance, before turning to the following villagers.

"Thank you all. You've all been a great help. We'll look after her, now. So, please go home quietly." With that, they turned away and headed down the road towards the church yard.

Pritchard remained and, although he played along by joining in the natural euphoria and release of emotions shown by the villagers before they began to drift away, he was also looking around him to see what Jones' reaction had been to Ali's entrance. But Jones was nowhere to be seen. Jones had gone!

Chapter Twenty-Two

Lieutenant Jennings' platoon had made good time in reaching London Road and was able to tuck in behind a small convoy of American army trucks heading towards Beckhampton. As if to help them further, another convoy closed up behind them and their journey up to Baltic was made in one, long column of vehicles without attracting undue attention. So, when the time came for the platoon to peel off at its destination onto a track, prior to dispersal, Jennings felt relaxed that the first part of the exercise had gone as planned.

The driver of the lorry following them gave him a 'thumbs up' as he went past and then closed up with trucks ahead.

In preparing for the exercise, Jennings had noted (with Pritchard's reminder) that the Baltic site was bounded on two sides by features which would help his mission. Along the northern side, about six hundred yards away, ran an old Roman road – now an open farm track bordered by sporadic stunted bushes – while, a half-mile to the west, was the Wansdyke, a deep, ancient ditch with high embankments which ran for miles across the windswept downs.

Jennings pulled off the track and the vehicles climbed the outer embankment of the Wansdyke and descended steeply to the bottom of the ditch. There they stopped beside a collection of bushes and, within minutes, they had merged into the landscape beneath camouflage netting.

The men then gathered round while Jennings used a stick to draw a rough map of their surroundings on the ground and pointed out the positions they were to occupy.

"When you reach your posts it is vital that you conceal yourselves. There's very little cover up here, as you can see, so that's not going to be easy. So use every scrap of vegetation and ground feature you can find. Rub soil onto your faces and stuff your helmet netting and webbing with any grass or plants that are handy."

The men all nodded.

"And remember," continued Jennings, "we are expecting someone to be approaching across country from here and heading for the barn over here." He jabbed the locations with his stick.

"So, at some point, they will have to pass through our lines. So it's vital you can't be seen from any angle. If this person gets so much as a sniff of our presence, we are buggered!"

The men again nodded, clearly ready to disperse.

"We don't know when or where this will happen, but it's likely this person will be coming from the village we've just passed, although we can't be certain of that. As for the time, it's also likely to happen at around dusk. So we've got to be on our toes."

Jennings looked up at the thunderclouds which were coming ever closer. "And, seeing this weather approaching, dusk may come early this evening. Now, once the person has passed through our lines, no one must be allowed to pass back through our cordon until you receive further orders. Is that clear? "

Again they nodded and he looked at the circle of eager faces. "You've trained well, chaps, and I know you'll give a good account of yourselves. Now get to your positions."

Following Pritchard's instructions, Jennings sent Corporal Parker and his two crewmen in the Bren gun carrier along the old Roman road, crossing London Road by the sheep pens, to take up a position at the end of the grass landing strip.

To the west of Baltic, the long grass on the banks of the Wansdyke gave excellent cover and ten soldiers were sent there to conceal themselves at intervals along its length. Five men were sent to cover the north side of the farm from the Roman road, while Jennings took the scout car and the remainder of the platoon back across the road to provide an arc of cover on the downs to the south of the barn and the airstrip. Once they'd camouflaged the vehicle beside a solitary clump of blackthorn bushes, they concealed themselves in the long, downland grass and prepared to wait.

Baltic was now surrounded.

From below the Hollow, Pritchard had watched Jennings' progress with quiet satisfaction as the convoy had made its way slowly along the road above the village before it disappeared over the hill and he calculated the platoon would be in position within the next thirty minutes.

He called up Captain Masters on the radio and reported the situation. "I should be joining you in around ten minutes," he said and the captain confirmed her guards would be looking out for him.

He was in the process of stowing the mike back under the dash when he spotted a movement in the driving mirror and he instinctively drew his revolver. But, when he turned to see what had caught his attention, he was surprised to see Ali Jenkins pulling up by the car on her bicycle, so he quickly replaced the gun and opened the door to greet her.

He gave her a hug and a quick kiss. "I didn't expect to see you here," he said. Then, holding her at arm's length, he looked at her clothing. "And I certainly didn't expect to see you in those clothes." Ali was now wearing dark-coloured slacks and sweater, with a tweed cap on her head.

"Well, a dress isn't very practical for crawling through the countryside," she replied, breathless from her cycling, "so I had just time to go home to change and catch up with you, before you left for Baltic."

"But you surely aren't expecting to come with me?"

"I certainly am," replied Ali, defiantly.

"But, Ali, please see reason. That could be exposing you to considerable danger – even more danger than you've already been through!" He smiled understandingly at her. "Don't you see? I don't want you putting yourself at risk again."

Ali's body stiffened with resentment.

"Hang on, Peter," she objected, "I'm grateful for your concern but you seem to have forgotten that I've been as much involved in this business as anybody – *and* I've been attacked by this Nazi bastard *and* lost a dear friend in the process. I've earned the right to be in this operation."

Pritchard realised further argument would waste valuable time. He looked at his watch and frowned. "You're putting me in difficult position, you know." He took just a moment to decide. "Right, hop in!"

Abandoning her bike by the churchyard wall, Ali ran round to the passenger door and jumped in as Pritchard started the engine and the car pulled away.

"Aren't you going to be too hot in those clothes?" he asked, looking over at her.

"They're a bit warm at the moment, I admit," answered Ali, glancing up through the window at the sky, "but, if this storm breaks, it could be a lot cooler later on." So saying, Ali wound down the window to let in a hot, but welcome, breeze into the car.

Pritchard frowned. "Now listen to me carefully," he said. "Captain Masters will be briefing us when we get to Baltic and, no matter how you may be feeling, it's her show. Her team will have things under control and I don't want you getting mixed up in her arrangements. Please promise me that!"

"Don't worry, Peter. I'll keep out of the way," she said. She wanted to add, "unless I'm wanted." However, the gleam in her eye and her tone of voice couldn't hide her determination, and it didn't go undetected by Commander Pritchard.

At the top of The Hollow, Pritchard had to wait for yet another line of trucks to pass before he was able to pull out onto London Road. He was forced to follow at the convoy's speed, which slowed occasionally to overtake farm-workers cycling home, so it wasn't until a further ten minutes that he was able to turn off onto the chalk track to the farm.

When they reached the row of beech trees, two armed soldiers stepped out from the shadows of the tree line and waved them to a halt.

"Commander Pritchard to see Captain Masters," he told the guard.

"Very good, sir. We've been expecting you," replied the sergeant. "But can I see your ID please, sir?"

Pritchard smiled and produced his ID card which the guard examined closely, while his corporal colleague hung a few paces back, his Sten gun slung at the ready.

The sergeant handed back the card and then he looked across at Ali.

"And who's this person, sir? We have orders to admit just you, sir."

"This is Alison Jenkins, Sergeant. She works for me and I can vouch for her," Pritchard explained.

The sergeant was unimpressed and the other soldier quietly moved a pace closer and raised his weapon.

"Sorry, sir. We got strict instructions that only you was to be allowed to pass."

Ali felt uneasy that her insistence to accompany Pritchard had caused him a problem at such a critical time.

"Then would you please use your radio, Sergeant, and get your clearance for Miss Jenkins to come in with me," instructed Pritchard, sharply. "She is known to Captain Masters."

The sergeant bent down and looked across at Ali again before saying to Pritchard, "Very good, sir. If you wouldn't mind staying here, sir. I'll go and check."

He marched quickly back to the trees, where he could be seen using his walkie-talkie and looking back across to them, while the Corporal remained motionless in front of the car with his Sten gun raised.

A few minutes later, the Sergeant returned. "Sorry about that, sir. That's all in order now. Miss Jenkins can proceed with you."

"Thank you, Sergeant," said Pritchard, who was about to move off when the sergeant again raised his hand.

"Sorry, sir. I still need to see Miss Jenkins' I.D.."

Ali fumbled in her pocket and produced her card for the Sergeant to scrutinise closely, before passing it back to her.

"Thank you, miss. That's fine." He then turned to Pritchard. "Now, if you'd follow the road round to the buildings, sir." The corporal then relaxed, lowered his weapon and stood aside, while the sergeant waved them through.

The clouds to the east had advanced with gathering speed and had grown much darker. Their progress was accompanied by louder, more frequent and closer rumbles of thunder. In the west, the low, setting sun directed an almost theatrical light underneath the clouds, before it was finally blotted out. Daylight was fading rapidly.

The breeze which had sprung up earlier now freshened and the first drops of rain for nearly two weeks began to fall. At first, they could be heard more than felt and the air was filled with that smell which reminded Private Smithson, stationed on the Wansdyke, of the market garden hothouses where he used to work.

The sounds around Smithson had changed since he'd taken up his post, lying flat on his stomach. At first, the most prominent noise had been the rustle of the downland grasses being waved gently to and fro in the breeze beside his head while, above him, a flock of peewits continuously circled noisily. He could even hear the occasional rattle of debris as a rabbit behind him scampered across the scree of chalky soil in front of the many burrows in the embankment.

But, as the strength of the wind increased, the grass movement around him became more frenzied, threshing like waves in a sea, as the air rushed through it with the same loud, whistling shriek which had swept the downs for millennia. To add to this hostility, a vivid flash of lightning lit up the terrain ahead of him, followed closely by a crack of thunder, immediately overhead.

Private Smithson huddled down under his waterproof cape and trained his rifle sights yet again on the barn as the large, fat raindrops steadily increased to a torrent.

The sound he heard first was indistinct – over to his right. But this was followed by the crackling sound of someone treading on dry vegetation behind and below him and Private Smithson froze, his heart thumping as he tried to flatten himself still further into the ground. Then, despite the noises of wind and rain, he heard the sound of heavy breathing as someone struggled to climb up the slippery slope of the embankment just to Smithson's left.

"Bloody hell!" he thought. "This bugger's right on top of me!" He remained motionless and prayed fervently that he wouldn't be discovered. Surely, the intruder was going to step on him if he didn't actually see him.

For some minutes, there were no further sounds, except those of the storm, and Smithson at first thought that the intruder had left. Then, suddenly, there was a loud grunt of exertion accompanied by the sound of feet scrabbling on wet grass as the intruder pulled himself up the steep embankment and onto the top, where he stood up, panting heavily. At that moment, there was a brilliant flash of lightning and Smithson got a clear picture of a man, standing in a wet, saturated mackintosh. A moment later, there was a peal of thunder like tearing calico and, when the lightning next flashed, the man had gone.

Inside the barn there was a warm silence. Everyone lay in readiness, submerged in loose straw and concealed behind bales. The only pervading sound was the faint roar of the rain, which was now falling in torrents on the tiled roof.

Pritchard and the Controller had discussed the prospects of the evening with Captain Masters before they had left the farmhouse.

"This whole thing could be a wild goose chase," the Controller confided in Masters, looking rather depressed. "We've absolutely no proof that he's coming here. And even if he planned to take your plane, he'd surely not risk trying to fly it in these conditions."

"I shouldn't comment on the first part, sir, although, from your intelligence, everything points to him coming here," she replied brightly. "But, if he was looking for conditions to cover his leaving the village, this evening's weather couldn't have given him a better opportunity. Our MET information shows that this storm will take less than an hour to pass through. After that, flying conditions are likely to be ideal." She looked round the faces. "Don't worry. If he's an experienced pilot, he'll know that, too."

"But what about starting it?" asked Ali. "Would he know what to do?"

"Our plane is a Lysander which has been specially modified for our operations with space for three passengers, at a pinch, and another allows cockpit starting. The rest of the controls, I'm told, are quite conventional." She looked at Ali. "So, yes, he'd find it easy enough to start."

The others all nodded.

"And what length of runway would he need to get airborne?" asked Pritchard.

"Unloaded? That'd be possible in just a hundred and fifty yards," she answered.

"Strewth," exclaimed Pritchard, "no wonder you find it a useful tool."

Captain Masters smiled. "Yes, it's brilliant for our purposes and we've relied on it to get us out of plenty of scrapes."

"So what would be the procedure for getting the plane out of the barn and ready to fly?" the Controller asked Masters.

"The sequence he'd need to follow would be to open the barn doors to their full extent. The doors are normally locked but, tonight, we've been uncharacteristically lax with our security, so he should have no problem there. Next he'd have to find the plane under the straw and netting. He'd need to remove that before he could push the plane outside to the hard standing."

"Would that be difficult?" asked Pritchard.

"It usually takes two of my ground crew to do that but one man would manage it after a struggle," she replied.

"Could he then just jump in and fly off?" asked Ali in a worried tone.

"Theoretically, yes. But he'll know it's important to make some cockpit checks first and also to check the levels in the fuel tank. As he probably hasn't flown a Lysander before, he'd also need to familiarise himself with the controls layout. On top of that, he'd know he has to turn over the radial engine several times to prevent damaging it before starting up. So all of that could take him a good five minutes or so."

The Controller asked, "How long would the whole thing take? Start to finish."

Masters made a brief mental calculation. "I'd say between ten and fifteen minutes."

The Controller nodded his appreciation for this information. "That's excellent. In that case, we have ample time to arrest him and reclaim that package before he can head back to the Fatherland."

"Yes, but I'm just hoping that's possible without damaging my plane," said Masters. "It's vital for our operations."

Pritchard was keen to know about the reception arrangements that Captain Masters had made and, after hearing about her preparations, they all stepped out into the rain and headed for the barn.

The reception party lay motionless. It seemed an age since they'd taken up their places at strategic positions amongst the straw bales and their eyesight had now gradually adjusted to the dark interior since, although at first there was total blackness, faint sources of light, provided by chinks in the roof tiles and cracks in the weather boarding, provided sufficient light to recognise the outline shapes of the barn's contents and, with the passing of the storm clouds, visibility improved considerably.

Pritchard again looked at the luminous dial of his watch. It was seven-thirty and the platoon had been in position for well over an hour while, in the barn, they had been waiting for forty-five minutes. The only sound was the continuous moaning of the wind through the rafters high above them and the rustle of an occasional of mouse.

Ali, for whom waiting was not a strong point, thought that at least two hours must have passed.

The Commander was beginning to question his own judgement and wrestled in his mind with the sequence of decisions he'd sanctioned which now culminated in their present vigil.

He, too, checked his watch. His presumptions had clearly been wrong, he conceded, and he must give the command to abort the mission.

At that precise moment they all heard the unmistakable sound of someone attempting to open the barn doors...

Chapter Twenty-Three

One of the barn doors slid back just a few inches. The intruder was clearly having difficulty in moving its massive weight. After some more scraping sounds, the door slid back further to make a gap wide enough for someone to squeeze through and, at the same time, allowing light to come flooding into the barn's interior.

The members of the reception party tensed in anticipation, their weapons trained on the gap when through it stepped the figure of a small boy.

Ali gasped when she recognised him. It was Alfie Barter! "What in hell's name is he doing here?" she groaned silently to herself, and she was about to stand up and yell at him to get out of sight when, with a rumble, the big door slowly resumed its opening progress.

Startled by the noise behind him, Alfie whirled round to see the cause and stepped back a few paces into the barn in alarm as the door continued to trundle towards being fully open.

Terrified at being discovered, Alfie turned and ran and dived behind some straw bales, only to find he was staring into the face of Ali Jenkins, who was lying there in the straw and cradling a gun.

Ali shot out a hand to cover his mouth and, releasing her gun, motioned with a finger to her lips to stay silent.

Ashen faced, Alfie was too shocked to move, except to nod vigorously.

"Don't move an inch!" hissed Ali and, again, he nodded. "And not a sound!"

Only then did she slowly remove her hand from the frightened boy's face and, cradling her gun again, she looked back to the half-open barn entrance.

Into the gap left by the door strode the figure of Roger Jones, silhouetted against the bright evening light, as if on the stage of some theatrical drama. Pritchard had seen the prompt action taken by Ali and prayed that Jones hadn't spotted Alfie as he'd squeezed inside the barn ahead of him. It seemed that, on this occasion, his prayers were not to be answered.

"Alfie! Hello, Alfie!" called Jones and he listened for a reply. When he wasn't answered, he called out again, this time a little louder, his voice echoing round the barn.

"Hello! Alfie! I know you're in here somewhere. Remember, we met after that plane crash." When there was still no response, he gave a short laugh and resorted to the call that children sang out in a game of hide and seek.

"Come out, come out wherever you are." Still he got no answer. He repeated his song. "Come out, come out, wherever you are."

The Controller lay covered in straw and concluded with relief that Jones' confident behaviour meant he could have no inkling that his escape plans had been rumbled.

Jones stood still, listening intently for any sound that might betray Alfie's whereabouts, but the echoing barn remained silent. Then Jones resorted to a different approach.

"Come on, Alfie. You can help me uncover my aeroplane. You like aeroplanes, don't you, Alfie? You can give me a hand." He paused, and then added, "If you're really good, I'll let you sit in the cockpit."

When he still got no answer, he appeared to abandon the thought of getting Alfie to reveal himself and he proceeded to investigate the camouflaged plane.

Captain Masters had ensured that it was less than thoroughly concealed and Jones made easy work of pulling off the tarpaulins, netting and straw which covered the craft. This resulted in clouds of dust, which was picked up by the shafts of light projecting through the cracks in the barn walls, like some rustic cinema.

Jones brushed down his clothes in an attempt to remove the fine dust which he'd disturbed. He could now see the black Lysander was pointing into the barn and he realised he'd either have to push it out backwards or, alternatively, swing it round to exit the barn frontwards.

His first option quickly proved too difficult because the small tail wheel dug into the loose straw and debris which covered the barn floor. So he resorted to lifting and swinging the tail round in instalments, until the plane faced outwards. This was no easy task and he was only able to complete this after expending considerable effort.

Breathing heavily, Jones then strode across to the other door and began to slide it back to reveal the full width of the entrance.

Throughout these stages, he remained under the unwavering scrutiny of the reception party, the members lying motionless in their hiding places.

Panting from his exertions, Jones then went back to the plane and rested, leaning on the bulbous fuel tank which was slung between the arms of the undercarriage.

When he had eventually recovered his breath, he checked the fuel level and gave a grunt of satisfaction at finding that the tank was full.

Looking on from his vantage point, Pritchard saw that Jones seemed to be in no particular hurry in his preparations and he watched him as he next walked round to the front of the plane and inspected the engine. He then climbed up to open the hatch to the pilot's cockpit to check that the ignition was turned off before climbing back down and returning to the front of the plane. Then, reaching up to catch hold of the first of the three propeller blades, he began to turn the engine over, just as Captain Masters had predicted.

When he'd turned the engine over several times he appeared to hesitate, as if mentally checking that, in the process of preparing for his flight, he'd not overlooked any essential item. He walked round the black plane, checking to his satisfaction the rudder, the flaps and ailerons.

If the tension among those watching these preparations had heightened, they showed no sign of it.

Pritchard was keeping one eye on Captain Masters, on whose command the final act of the operation depended, but she remained motionless and unmoved.

After Jones had finished his inspection he buttoned up his coat and, as if to assure himself that his preparations were at last complete, he patted his pockets and, out of one, he drew a Luger pistol while, out of the other, he pulled out a package which Ali and Sharples immediately recognised. He replaced the gun and the package deep into the safety of his coat pockets and turned in readiness to climb up into the cockpit.

It was then that Alfie Barter succumbed to the straw dust which hung in the air and gave a loud sneeze.

Jones whirled round in surprise but then regained his composure. His produced his pistol, which he hung loose at his side and took several steps towards the straw bales from which the sound had come.

"Come out, Alfie! Come on. You know that no one's going to hurt you."

Ali was just thinking that, if Jones came any closer, she'd be seen when, inexplicably, Alfie stood up and walked out from behind the bales where he'd been hiding.

"Ah, there you are!" greeted Jones. "You know, Alfie, you're a fine strong boy and, if you'd been born in my country, you'd now be an important member of the Hitler Youth. D'you know that?"

He gave the boy an encouraging smile. "Yes, you'd have a smart uniform and a dagger all of your own." He smiled again at Alfie, who was bewildered by what Jones was saying. "I could take you with me, Alfie, if you like. The German *Reich* needs boys like you." Jones waved towards the plane. "Would you like to come with me, Alfie?"

Alfie started to walk slowly towards Jones and, for an agonising moment, Pritchard thought he was going to accept Jones' invitation. Then Alfie made to move past him when Jones raised his gun and waved it menacingly at the boy.

"Alfie! Stay exactly where you are!"

The boy looked at Jones and then at the gun in his hand.

"I aint goin' in that plane with you, if that's what you think," he said, defiantly. "An' I heard you went an' killed that teacher woman," he said, abruptly changing the subject.

Ali became even tenser. "What can the boy be thinking," she said to herself. "He's either extremely brave or he's being a bloody idiot."

"Oh, that," laughed Jones. "That was just very unfortunate. You see, she wouldn't do what she was told. So you see what happens to people if they don't do as I say, Alfie!"

"Bugger that!" said Alfie. "I aint a feared of you nor of no gun. I got to get home for my tea." And with that defiant retort, Alfie turned on his heel and made towards the barn door.

Jones raised his gun and aimed at the boy's head.

The next few seconds produced a blur of actions, but to Pritchard they appeared to happen in a slow motion sequence.

First, Ali leaped to her feet and screamed a warning to Alfie. Jones whirled round and levelled his gun at her. This was followed by streak of silver from the top of the bales and Jones screamed out in pain as the bolt from a crossbow smashed into his arm, his gun thumping to the floor.

Then the bales erupted as every member of the reception party leapt to their feet and, shaking off trails of straw and brandishing their weapons, they converged on the Nazi, who now writhed in pain on the floor, clutching his shattered arm and swearing in his mother tongue.

Pritchard ran to the man's side and yanked open his mouth. After a short struggle he succeeded in retrieving a small glass capsule, which Jones had been trying to swallow.

"Oh, no you don't," he said, with grim satisfaction. "We can't let a drop of cyanide deprive our justice system of its due process!"

Ali thrust her hand into Jones' coat pocket and triumphantly produced the precious package which she'd last held in Colin Sharples' room at Lynton House. Meanwhile, Pritchard deprived Jones of the Luger, which he handed to one of Captain Masters' team.

The Controller leant forward and lifted the package from her fingers. "I think I'd better take care of that." He then turned to the figure writhing on the floor.

"Colin Jones, or whatever your name really is, you are now under arrest for espionage and for the murders of a British subject and of a German national." The Controller looked down at him pitilessly. "You will be taken to a hospital to have your arm attended to and then on to a military prison to await your trial. I need hardly remind you of the penalty for both charges, if you are found guilty."

He turned to Captain Masters. "Captain, please get this piece of Nazi garbage out of my sight!"

Two hours later, the Controller, Pritchard and Ali Jenkins sat with Captain Masters and two members of her team around the kitchen table at Baltic farm, cradling mugs of hot tea and reliving the events of the evening.

Before he'd been taken home, Alfie Barter had been given a lecture on the dreadful and dire consequences that could befall a small boy, should he ever tell anyone of the events in the barn that evening.

The plane had been pushed back into the barn and both plane and barn had been camouflaged again.

Lieutenant Jennings' platoon had been ordered to stand down, with the Controller's congratulations and thanks, while Private Smithson had capitalised on his close encounter on the Wansdyke. His accounts of the evening became more exaggerated with each telling, as he profited from the extra fags and beers he was offered.

The Controller smiled the grim smile of satisfaction. "I'll be the first to admit that I'm relieved about the way things have turned out tonight." Everyone nodded and sipped their tea. "It was a first class show, particularly since we couldn't be certain that Jones would show up like he did."

"Yes, there were a number of things we couldn't have predicted," added Pritchard. "That boy, for instance, turning up like he did! For a moment back there, I was certain our plans would be scuppered."

"I still can't think what came over him to act in the way that he did," said Ali. "He knew that if Jones had come any further into the barn, I would have been discovered. Was he trying to save me, d'you think?"

Pritchard smiled at Ali. "Who knows what goes on in that head of his? There may be some truth in what you say, Ali, but I don't think he really appreciated the danger he was placing himself in. All he thought was that he'd been caught in a place where he knew he shouldn't be – just like being caught scrumping in Mrs Rumain's orchard by PC Harper."

"Whatever his motives, we owe young Barter a debt of gratitude," concluded the Controller. "Thanks to him, we've bagged a dangerous Nazi agent. And while we're all here, I'm sure we all want to see this."

The Controller had delved into his pocket and produced the package which had been the focus of all their efforts for what had seemed a very long time.

"Let's just have a look at what we've deprived the Third Reich from receiving."

He carefully unwrapped the package and spread the contents over the table. In addition to the German passport, there were three sheets of paper covered in minute German writing, two pages of drawings of electrical circuitry, and a miniature camera.

The Controller pushed the pages of German text across the table. "Captain Masters, you're our linguist. Any idea what these sheets are about?"

Rosemary Masters collected a magnifier from a shelf and examined the sheets carefully while the others waited expectantly.

"Well," she said, at last, "Mr Jones has been a very busy boy! This first part lists in detail the build up of Allied troops in the area. There is a list of American companies and British regiments, which are stationed at Devizes, Warminster and Tidworth with estimated strength of numbers for each. There is another list. This one gives details of allied planes which are operational at the RAF stations at Keevil, Colerne, Upavon, Melksham and Lyneham. A third list includes details of operations at the R.A.F. stations at Yatesbury and Amesbury." She paused. "There's even reference to civilian morale and the impact of food and petrol rationing. However, I'm pleased to see there's no mention of my operation here or of the GHQ Auxiliary."

"Good God!" exclaimed Pritchard. "He had a complete picture of all of our principal concentrations of military hardware around here. If the German High Command got their hands on this information, it could scupper any Allied plans for an invasion of Europe."

"Yes, and I suspect these drawings are of the circuitry for the RDF development at Horton Lab," confirmed Masters. "I'd hate to think of the consequences, had Germany got hold of these. As it is, it looks likely that RDF could go a long way to help us to get the upper hand in this war, at last."

"Quite so, Captain," said the Controller, who was looking closely at the miniature camera. "As for this little fellow, we'll have to wait for the film to be developed, but my guess is it will contain still more sensitive information connected to the War effort."

The Controller waved his hands above the papers which lay on the table. "In any event, we've not only prevented this information from leaving the country but we have here plenty of ammunition for the prosecution."

"What's likely to happen to Jones?" asked Captain Masters. "I presume he's hardly the sort of agent that you could 'turn', as you put it, Commander."

"Absolutely not!" replied Pritchard, shaking his head. "He's been too deeply indoctrinated with Nazi dogma and he's steeped in their cause. He's also a double murderer, a combination which hardly makes him suitable material."

"No," joined the Controller. "I've no doubt that Herr Jones will be found guilty, so I think we all know what his fate is likely to be."

The Controller's face looked drawn and tired from the evening's events and, turning to Pritchard, he said, "Now, these drawings. They need to be returned to Horton Lab. I'm not sure if the drawings are the original documents or copies, but I'm certain their return would be welcomed."

Prichard nodded. "I'll take care of that, sir. You can leave that to me."

"There's one loose end we still haven't cleared up," said Ali, "and that's Richard Kymer. What has he been up to? Remember, he lied about his background, he reckoned he'd been invalided out of the army and he had a coil of wire hanging in his room, which all seemed fishy to me." She looked at Pritchard. "At one stage, I thought he might have been our man. You were going to check up on him, Peter?"

"Yes, well Mr Kymer was, indeed, injured at Catterick during army training – but not under that name. His real name is Richard Schultz and he's a German national who fled Germany, along with other Jews fleeing persecution. However, with a name like that, he knew he'd no chance of getting employment in the present climate and there was the possibility of him being interned for the duration on the Isle of Man, which he wanted to avoid at all costs."

"So he changed his name?"

"That's right. He had been an apprentice at a German radio manufacturer when war broke out and he was an avid shortwave radio enthusiast. Although strictly illegal, he'd kept his equipment and the wire you found was his aerial. Sadly for him, he's had his stuff impounded, so he won't be searching the airwaves any more."

Captain Masters cleared her throat. "Controller, if you'll excuse me, I've got to prepare for an insertion first thing tomorrow morning, so I'll leave you now."

"Thank you, Captain. Of course go ahead. We are all indebted to you and to your team for your efforts this evening." He looked at Ali and Pritchard. "I think we've all had a long day so, let's leave Captain Masters to it."

So, with a scraping of chairs, everyone stood up ready to leave. The Controller, followed by Pritchard and then Ali, shook Masters' hand and bade her goodnight, as they made their way out of the farmhouse. Ali looked back at her and called, "And have a safe trip."

Masters smiled and waved in return. They all knew she would be taking risks on their behalf, with no certainty of a safe return.

The driver opened the car door for the Controller, who turned to Ali and Pritchard. "D'you know? I think our fortunes in this war are beginning to take a turn for the better. God knows, we could do with some good news." He looked towards the distant barn, which was barely visible through the evening dusk. "And what you two have achieved over the past few weeks has been quite remarkable."

Prichard and Ali smiled back at him.

The Controller got into his car and wound down the rear window. "What have you got planned now, Commander?"

Pritchard smiled at Ali. "Well, some time ago I had promised to give Miss Jenkins a thorough briefing on the intelligence service but I never managed to get round to it. So I think this evening would be as good a time as any."

The Controller smiled at them and waved goodbye, as his car drove out of the farmyard.

Once in their car, Ali looked across at Prichard with an impish smile. "Well, Commander. I'm looking forward to this briefing."

"So am I," replied Pritchard, with a laugh. "And I can promise you it will be detailed and extremely thorough!"

They drove out of the yard, turned onto the road and headed back towards the village.